What's Wrong,
Who's Right
in
CENTRAL AMERICA?

What's Wrong, Who's Right in CENTRAL AMERICA?

Second Edition

Richard A. Nuccio
Roosevelt Center for American Policy Studies

Holmes & Meier   New York / London

Second edition published in the United States of America 1989 by
Holmes & Meier Publishers, Inc.
30 Irving Place
New York, NY 10003

Library of Congress Cataloging-in-Publication Data

Nuccio, Richard.
  What's wrong, who's right in Central America?

  Bibliography: p.
  Includes index.
  1. Central America—Politics and government—
1979– . I. Title.
F1439.5.N83 1986   972.8'053
ISBN 0-8419-1177-0 (alk. pa.)

To my son, Erin, who makes it all worthwhile

To my parents, who believed in the higher education
they never had the opportunity to pursue,
and to my grandmother,
who made it possible for me

Contents

Preface to the Second Edition   ix

Preface to the First Edition   xiii

Prologue
El Salvador: No Neutral Ground   xvii
Nicaragua: Capturing the Private Sector   xviii

1   *Central America from Columbus to Castro*   1

2   *Central American "Snapshots"*   47

3   *Five Countries and Ten Questions: The Policy Debate*   91

4   *The Politics of Central American Policy*   137

Index   163

Preface to the Second Edition

In the three years since *What's Wrong, Who's Right in Central America?* first appeared, the grim statistics about Central America have only continued to mount. The death toll from civil wars and other forms of political violence in Guatemala, El Salvador, Nicaragua, and Honduras has increased; Costa Rica remains an island of democratic virtue, but one where indices of poverty are rising; and Panama, left out of the first edition because it seemed to have avoided the problems afflicting the rest of Central America, is not included in this edition because it would require another book to describe the near-collapse of that society's economic and political order.

Some five years ago the Roosevelt Center was concerned that the combination of an administration preoccupied with Central America as a region in which U.S. resolve would be tested, and a public that was apathetic and largely uninformed about the most basic aspects of U.S. Central American policy, was unlikely to produce a consistent, coherent, or successful policy for the region. That concern was, unfortunately, confirmed by the conflict between the executive and legislative branches that culminated in the so-called Iran-Contra affair, and by the fact that President Bush will be confronted with the necessity of constructing a new bipartisanship on virtually all aspects of U.S. policy in the region. He will also face the fact that after eight years of the most intense media, government, academic, church, labor, and interest-group efforts to "educate" the North American public on Central America:

- more citizens think El Salvador is an unfriendly country or an enemy of the United States (43%) than perceive it as a friendly country or an ally of the United States (32%);

- more citizens believe that El Salvador has a pro-Soviet communist government (35%) than think it has a democratic government (15%) (one-third are not sure what type of government El Salvador has); and

- a 61% majority of citizens polled say the Soviet Union is supporting a communist revolution against the government of Nicaragua.*

The good news is that in the last five years the Roosevelt Center has confirmed that the same kind of citizens reached in these polls can come to reasoned and reasonable judgments about U.S. policy in Central America if they are given the opportunity to spend even a few hours with balanced material on the region that outlines the basic options facing U.S. policy. In a simulation on Central America designed by the center to introduce adults and students to Central American politics and U.S. policy toward the region called *Bullets & Ballots,* thousands of participants in the center's programs across the country have come together with fellow-citizens of different political orientations to debate their preferred solutions to the conflicts of Central America. Playing the roles of army generals, peasants and workers, U.S. officials, or guerrilla fighters, they have confronted the legacies of violence, injustice, and suspicion that drive Central American politics, and have taught themselves about the obstacles to peaceful solutions. Observing these citizens in countless events across the country I have come away more enthusiastic than ever about the—so far unrealized—potential of the general public for meaningful participation in the debate over Central America. It would be yet another tragedy of U.S. foreign policy and a disservice to this public if the weariness in Washington over Central America and the presumed preference of the electorate for attention to domestic priorities were to lead to a new period of malign neglect of Central America.

Americans Talk Security: A Survey of Attitudes Concerning National Security Issues, National Survey no. 5, "Public Perceptions and Attitudes Affecting Opinions of U.S. Policy in Central America and U.S. Drug Problem and Foreign Policy Implications (May 1988).

This second edition represents a significant revision and update. Major changes have been made in chapters 2 and 3 to reflect the evolving situation in each of the countries. Chapter 4 deals with the domestic politics of the Central American policy process and is completely new.

In addition to those I acknowledged in the first edition to this book I should like to add thanks to Michael Shifter and Louis Goodman whose comments came in time to save some unwise judgments from appearing in the text, but not in time for them to be included in the preface. Max Holmes and my editor, Barbara Lyons, of Holmes & Meier made this second edition at an accessible paperback price an unexpected reality. Special thanks go to Marta Tannenhaus who worked so effectively during the "public engagement" phase of the Central America project and who contributed in many ways to this second edition, most directly in the section on "Iran-Contra: An Affair to Remember."

Finally, I want to thank Angelina Ornelas for loving me so well during these last years.

Richard A. Nuccio
December 1988

Preface to the
First Edition

Central America is not just for specialists. It should be of concern to everyone who cares about the issues of peace and war. In Central America organized violence by forces of the right and left has cost the lives of over 100,000 people during the last seven years. President Reagan has defined what happens in the region as of vital interest to the United States. Yet opinion polls continue to confirm that nearly three-fourths of those questioned do not know which side the United States supports—the government or its armed opposition—in the key countries of El Salvador and Nicaragua.

What's Wrong, Who's Right in Central America? was not written to support or to oppose official policy in Central America. It is designed to provide average citizens with basic information and analysis that will allow them to make their own judgments about what U.S. policy in the region should be. The Roosevelt Center, as a nonpartisan, nonadvocacy institution, has no particular axe to grind in the making of U.S. Central American policy. But we do believe that what happens in that part of the world will affect the future of U.S. relations with all of Latin America and help to determine how the United States will deal with social change in Third World countries—a challenge that will confront U.S. foreign policy for decades to come.

The organization of the book merits a brief comment. This introduction to Central America begins with two vignettes designed to paint a verbal picture of two very different kinds of realities in El

Salvador and Nicaragua. Chapter 1 is the briefest of summaries of
the history of the entire Central American region up to the 1970s.
Chapter 2 focuses on the five individual countries of Nicaragua, El
Salvador, Honduras, Costa Rica, and Guatemala in "snapshots"
that update political developments to late 1985. Chapter 3 is a
guide to the policy debate as it occurs in Washington for each of the
five countries told from the perspectives of a "national security
analyst" and a "human rights activist." Chapter 4 gives some
examples of how citizens have organized themselves to support or
oppose current policy toward Central America.

This book owes a debt to a great many people, only some of
whom can be acknowledged. Howard Wiarda, who taught my first
class on Latin American politics, and many thereafter, is probably
quoted verbatim at times in Chapter 1 without my knowing it!
Abraham Lowenthal was an early guide to holding conflicting ideas
in one's head simultaneously even before I had the chance to see
him do it firsthand during his stewardship of the Latin American
Program at the Wilson Center. Amando de Miguel, the Spanish
sociologist, showed me that "popularizing" ideas did not necessarily
demean them. All of these mentors thought I had a book in me; it
was a long time getting out.

Numerous friends and colleagues read early drafts of the manuscript. William LeoGrande and Virginia Polk were particularly generous with their time and were constructively critical. Carlos Egan
made detailed comments and posed some hard questions as only a
good friend can. Peter Hakim gave attention to substance and style.
Cynthia Arnson lent her considerable expertise on El Salvador.
Alexander Wilde helped defeat an unwise tentative title. As should
be evident to anyone who knows these individuals, their often
conflicting advice could not always be incorporated. But they
helped to keep me on track and to avoid most, but not all, errors.

My colleagues at the Roosevelt Center provided just the right
combination of carrot and stick to produce the book only slightly
behind schedule. Christopher Makins, director of international security studies, made detailed comments and offered broad encouragement. If his proper British demeanor permitted it, I would give
him a warm Latin *abrazo*.

Kelly McBride, director of research for the project, kept the pile
of Central America material flowing across my desk and into files

where it could be retrieved. She added her own firsthand experience in El Salvador and Nicaragua to Chapters 2 and 4. She worked closely with me on the design and conception of the book and her contributions are greatly appreciated.

Chris Namerdy put much of the original manuscript onto the word processor and helped to coordinate its production. Roger Kittleson was an invaluable intern during the last hectic phases of the book.

Thanks are especially due to the many Central Americans who offered their insights and experiences to a curious gringo, as well as to Janet Shenk, my first guide to the intrigues of Central America. Impressions gathered during that first visit contributed to the vignettes with which the book begins.

Richard A. Nuccio
December 1985

Prologue

El Salvador: No Neutral Ground

The refugee camp outside San Martín del Campo holds 5,000 human souls in barely human conditions. Houses are thatched huts with packed earthen floors supported by wooden poles. Foul water comes from a single pipe at the end of a muddy pathway; bathrooms are ditches cut in the dirt at the edge of the camp.

María is a leader of sorts in the camp. She has lived in one of these huts for nearly three years, since she fled the war in the eastern province of her country. She has special responsibilities as *botiquín,* the dispenser of basic medicines to combat diarrhea and the tubercular coughs that afflict many, especially the old. Being a *botiquín* is dangerous for María: she has medicine, a valuable commodity, and the local soldiers will always wonder if she passes it on to the subversives. She gets her supplies from the local religious lay workers; the army thinks they are subversives too.

As María talks, an eleven-month-old with a dirty face and only a tee-shirt for clothing toddles back and forth across the hut, crawling into his mother's lap to suck at her breast from time to time. He is the youngest of seven; the oldest is dead.

"He was a good boy, I still miss him so. He worked hard and tried to be someone. But they wouldn't leave him alone. He made friends with the police, and they taught him a skill. He learned to type, and each day he worked at the police station filling in reports on the machine. He typed so well and never made a mistake.

"But the guerrillas called him a collaborator, and one night they came and took him away. I don't know what they did to him there. He was not against the guerrillas, he was not for the police. We only want to live and work. We don't want to choose to fight and die.

"They kept him for two weeks. I didn't know what had happened to him. But they let him go or he escaped. People saw him coming down from the mountains. If he had come back, I would have made him leave here. Perhaps to go to the capital; maybe to try to make it to the United States. He was a good boy. He knew how to work hard.

"But he never made it back to us. A patrol of customs police saw him coming from the guerrilla area. They thought he was a subversive. They didn't believe that he was just my son, just a peasant boy, the joy of his mother. They tied his thumbs behind his back, and they shot him.

"Some say that death is peaceful. I do not believe that it is so. My son's face had the look of terror on it. I hope that God will give him the peace he did not have here. I hope that God will give us all peace."

Nicaragua: Capturing the Private Sector

The lunch of beans, rice, roasted pork, and salad was even more delicious taken in the sun-drenched courtyard of the coffeegrower's home. But we were not satisfied. The loyal coffeegrowers of Matagalpa had told us more of what we had been hearing from official spokespersons about the wonders of *Sandinismo*. We had come to this village birthplace of the Sandinista movement to meet with that elusive private sector, threatened but still surviving in "pluralist" Nicaragua. These men, owners of coffee plantations not nationalized by the government, represented the small-scale businesses that were being tolerated in Nicaragua's mixed economy of capitalism and socialism.

Some of the men looked and acted the part: uncomfortable in front of a group of foreigners, they seemed like hard-working farmer-entrepreneurs from any part of the world. Those who did the most talking, however, were clearly businessmen turned loyal politicians. Their praise of the revolution, with the familiar admission of "errors," seemed rehearsed. The members of our delegation shifted uneasily in their seats.

In the small groups that formed over lunch, we pressed some of the growers: Is everyone so enthusiastic about the Sandinistas? Could we meet growers who were not happy with the changes?

"Yes, perhaps that could be arranged," said one of the growers who had been especially quiet during the litany of praise. The largest grower in Matagalpa lived in town; he might be willing to see us.

The house of the richest grower was impressive even by North American standards. Constructed in Spanish style, its interior of tile and mosaic was cool and inviting. We seated ourselves next to a modern kitchen inside a room furnished with outdoor furniture. An expensive stereo played classical music in the background.

"I am the president of the coffeegrowers of this region and I have been a grower all my life. I have stayed in Nicaragua because this is my home. I did not allow Somoza to drive me from my home; I will not allow the Sandinistas to do it either.

"I am committed to the future. You saw the big Bank of America building on your way into town. I will borrow $100,000 from the Bank of America this year to plant new trees. These will not produce for a number of years. But if the Sandinistas let me, I will be here to pay off the loan.

"How is business? Not good. The government controls everything; my profits are worse than under Somoza. They tell me to whom I must sell and at what prices. Because of their fight with the United States, I can't get many of the imports I need. Sometimes I think that the government doesn't care about producing coffee. All they care about is Sandino.

"Yes, I criticize the government here in my home with Americans who need to know about our country. But it is dangerous. A friend's land was confiscated recently because he opposed the government. When you complain, they say you are a *contra* and take your land.

"But I still hope things will change. I don't like dictatorships of the right or the left. I want a free market, free schools, and a free church. When we were in Guatemala we had good church schools. Here they are trying to fill them up with Sandinista propaganda. And the church. There should be only one church for rich and poor. I don't believe in this people's church. Just one church.

"The poor are worse off now than they were under Somoza. Ask Pablito [the small grower who led us to the large grower's house and who now sits deferentially at his side]. He is a good worker; he rents land from me. Tell them how the peasants eat worse now than before."

"Well, Don Rodrigo, I'm not sure. You know, before there was much injustice and now the workers have at least the . . ."

"Nonsense, Pablito. The peasants were better off before the Sandinistas. On my farms we always had schools for the workers, took care of them, helped them when they had problems. Now they are worse off, don't you agree, Pablito?"

"Perhaps, Don Rodrigo, but also . . ."

"Absolutely. And if you say the truth they send the *turbas* [mobs] to attack you. You see that hole in the window? That is where the *turbas* attacked my house. This is *Sandinismo*."

As we leave the house, the young Nicaraguan lay worker for a Protestant church who has been accompanying us is downcast and sullen. The son of uneducated parents, he was identified at an early age as a natural leader and now at eighteen coordinates Protestant welfare projects throughout the northern provinces where he was born. Earlier in understated simplicity he had told us of the desperate conditions under which the poor with whom he works must live and how *Sandinismo* has meant improvement in the lives of many for the first time. Now his voice has an edge that we have not heard before.

"It was men like him who ruled my mother and father until they died. I grew up on a coffee plantation. We had no school; we had no doctor. People like him disgust me; they think they know everything. I wonder when he ever leaves this mansion to see how we peasants live on his wonderful farms?"

Months later, back in that other world called Washington, the note arrived. Our guide in Nicaragua thought we would want to know that the grower in whose house we shared lunch had been killed in the civil war. His severed head was left in the central plaza as a warning to others who collaborate with the Sandinistas. Perhaps we would want to protest the atrocity to the United States government which supports the opposition contras. Perhaps.

What's Wrong,
   Who's Right
   in
CENTRAL AMERICA?

1

Central America from Columbus to Castro

The "Black Legend" is about the original "evil empire." It is that set of truths, half-truths, and non-truths that the British created to justify their attacks on the Spanish empire many centuries ago. According to the "Black Legend," the Spanish were vile men possessed of evil notions of government who needed to be vanquished by the superior and enlightened British. All manner of outrages perpetrated by the British against the Spanish were legitimated by this "Black Legend."

The Spanish, for their part, came to view the Anglo-Saxons as the natural enemy of everything for which Spanish civilization stood. The fact that Catholic Spain saw itself as the defender of the true faith and that England was a defender of Protestantism made their enmity all the more bitter. From that time to the present day, the Spanish and their descendants have viewed with suspicion and hostility any criticism by Anglo-Saxons, including the North American variety, of their values and institutions. They see such criticism as a continuation of that "Black Legend" that had charged the Spanish with roasting heretics for breakfast.

To understand what is happening today in Central America, one must go back to the origins of these societies and to the values, attitudes, and institutions that Spain bequeathed to the nations of the New World. For North Americans it is helpful to contrast the founding of our own society in the seventeenth century with the

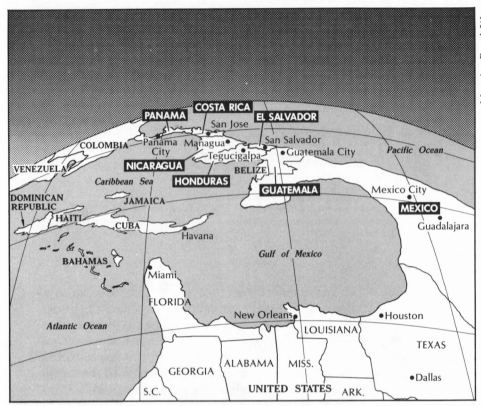

Map by Brad Wye

"Central America is America: it's at our doorstep."
—President Ronald Reagan, May 1984

founding of Latin America a century earlier. But it is important to do so without perpetuating the myths of the "Black Legend" that the "superiority" of the Anglo-Saxon race explains the different histories of Central America and the United States since each gained its independence.

Central Americans themselves have a certain ambivalence about their Spanish ancestors. Their societies would not exist in their current form were it not for the Spanish. Yet those societies were created as a result of the conquest of native peoples who in some parts of Central America had highly developed civilizations of their own. The traces of those native peoples can be seen in the faces of most of the inhabitants of Central America and heard in the myriad native languages that still prevail in many of the rural areas. The legacy of the destruction of these native civilizations is also evident in the land tenure system and the pattern of violence that make contemporary politics in Central America so vicious. The essence of Central America lies in its being a mixture of the Old World and the New.

The Founding of the Americas, North and South

The beginnings of what became the United States and the nations of Central America were very different. These two parts of the Americas were colonized more than a century apart and presented distinct environments to the colonizer. There were also differences in the characters of the men who came to the New World and in the values they brought with them.

Seventeenth-century England was a country on the verge of the social, political, and economic revolution—the Industrial Revolution—that created the modern world as we know it. English settlers in North America came from a modernizing England that generally treated literacy, toleration, individual rights, economic liberty, saving, and investment as inseparable elements of a process of change and growth. Sixteenth-century Spain was, on the other hand, a country struggling to emerge from the Dark Ages. Only recently reunited as a nation, Spain would spend the sixteenth and seventeenth centuries defending the traditional values of a monolithic Catholic Church, an authoritarian government, and an aristocratic order. While many English settlers in the New World came in search of religious freedom, Spanish conquerors imposed a purified Catholicism on the indigenous population.

The early settlers in North and South America encountered very different environments. The first English company charters provided for the discovery of precious-metal mines, but no mines were found. While Spanish conquerors to the south searched for El Dorado, the mythical city of gold, the English colonists established the small family farms that were suited to the ecology of the North American east coast. If the English had discovered mineral riches, they would have had no indigenous sources of labor to exploit them. Europeans in North America did not have to confront or incorporate substantial Indian cultures as was the case in much of

Central America. Indian culture was then, as it is today, irrelevant for the white society. The nomadic American Indian inhabitants were pushed aside, killed, or isolated as survivors on unproductive lands. The Spaniards, on the other hand, faced huge native populations that numbered in the tens of millions and lived a sedentary and, in some cases, highly civilized life. The temptation of the Spaniards to eliminate the native elite while leaving intact an authoritarian structure to exploit the rest of the population proved too great to resist.

These accidents of history had profound implications for the future of the two colonial areas. The story of Pocahontas, the Indian princess who converted to Christianity and married an Englishman, is part of North American mythology. But such an event was relatively rare. Because of the small numbers and nomadic existence of the North American Indians, white and Indian societies remained relatively isolated and racially distinct. In Mexico and Central America, the Spanish brought few women with them and intermarriage with the native population became commonplace. Demographic disaster from disease and brutal exploitation reduced the Indians' numbers dramatically in the first few decades after the conquest and set the stage for the creation of the distinctive *mestizo* (mixed) society that still characterizes parts of Central America today. In this *mestizo* society, a tiny Spanish elite ruled over a dwindling Indian peasantry and a growing, racially mixed lower and middle class. *Pureza de sangre* (purity of blood) became the trait that separated rich from poor, powerful from powerless. These racial divisions that became class and caste divisions would create barriers, which would not have to be faced in North America, to social mobility, income distribution, and to the very idea of national identity.

Nowhere in the New World except in North America did there exist a huge, accessible, underpopulated, virgin land of extraordinary resources that enjoyed a climate comparable to that of Europe. It was not surprising then that the North American colonists established different land tenure patterns from those in Central America.

The special social structure and land tenure pattern that characterized Central America was encouraged by the existence of a servile population suitable for slave labor, of mines that needed to be worked, and of a climate conducive to a plantation-type economy. Unlike the family farms of North America, Central America was characterized by large-scale enterprises that placed the privileged, white Spaniards in charge of the exploited native masses in mines, on *haciendas*,[1] and, eventually, on export-oriented plantations.

The pattern of these early economies had profound implications for the future political structures of the Central American countries. Mining and large-scale agriculture produced a two-class society where the few used political power to control and exploit the many. The middle class, so important in moderating tension between rich and poor in democratic countries, remained small and politically unimportant until well into the twentieth century in most of Central America. The monopoly of wealth held by the upper class distorted political development, as the Central American elite fought tooth and nail to resist change that would force them to share their power with those lower in the social scale.

In that part of North America most similar in climate to Latin America, the antebellum South, plantation economies based on the exploitation of imported slave labor did develop along with an aristocratic lifestyle and social differentiation of a racial kind. The tension between an industrial, relatively egalitarian North and an agricultural, slave-holding South eventually produced a cataclysmic civil war in the United States. One can gain some sense of the problems facing Central America today by speculating on what the United States would look like if the South rather than the North had won the war; if slavery, rather than being abolished, had been extended; and if the Southern aristocracy had maintained its political domination for ninety more years. Despite the crushing defeat of the South's social system in the Civil War, the heritage of slavery, racial discrimination, and plantation agriculture would continue to retard the development of the South for nearly a century. Only after the Second World War would the New South of industry and progress begin to emerge. Most of Latin America has never fought this kind of civil war to defeat a political and economic system based on the exploitation of peasant labor.

Central America entered the era of political independence with its colonial heritage bearing down on it. For a variety of internal and external reasons, societies had been created that were highly unequal and authoritarian, largely agricultural, and dependent on the outside world for many of the products necessary to their existence. It was not a propitious way to begin life as independent nations, and the manner in which that independence came to Central America set even more roadblocks on the path to a prosperous and democratic future.

Independence: Running Away from Change

Independence came to Mexico and Central America not as a struggle to preserve freedom from European tyranny, but as a way for conservative elites in the colonies to preserve their privileges from democratic reforms occurring in mother Spain. In Spain a Liberal constitution had been written in 1812 that provided for a limited monarchy, promised freedom of speech and assembly, and abolished the Inquisition. Initially suppressed by the Spanish King Ferdinand VII, the constitution was restored in 1820 and threatened to undermine the position of the colonial elite.

At the moment of independence, most Central American countries were divided into four distinct social groups. The *peninsulares,* or peninsulars, were native-born Spaniards whose purity of blood and connections to the crown gave them positions of privilege in the colonies in business, trade, and politics. The *criollos,* or creoles, were pure-blooded Spaniards who had been born in America and occupied the next rung of society. Ambitious and conscious of their social status, they resented the *peninsulares* and wished to replace them as the dominant group. *Ladinos,* or people of mixed blood, ranged in social status from a relatively well-off middle class to an impoverished underclass in the cities and rural areas. Aggressive and socially mobile, they formed the shock troops in the civil wars that were to follow independence. The Indians occupied the bottom rung of the social ladder and were abused and exploited by all those above them. Largely excluded from national economic and political life, they turned inward and focused on the family, the village, and the region.

Independence movements that had real mass support and promised to improve the lot of the Indians and *ladinos,* such as that led by Father Hidalgo in Mexico in 1810, were promptly and brutally put down by a coalition of *peninsulares* and *criollos.* Only when events in Spain raised the specter of change from above did the Mexican creole elite decide to back a movement for independence. In the region that became Central America, independence was even more half-hearted. A Mexican general, Iturbide, declared himself emperor of Mexico and threatened to "liberate" Central America by force in 1821. Faced with attack from without or a self-proclaimed independence, the future United Provinces of Central America declared independence.

With independence came the kind of bitter partisan debate that would consume Central America for the next thirty years. Different factions of the elite argued the merits of being an independent republic versus annexing themselves to Mexico. Once again events in Mexico forced decisions on the Central Americans. Iturbide's abdication in 1823 led to the proclamation of absolute Central American independence on July 1 of the same year. Only Chiapas elected to remain with Mexico to become the southernmost state of the Mexican federation.

The United Provinces of Central America, what we now know as Guatemala, Honduras, Nicaragua, El Salvador, and Costa Rica, began independent life with a number of strikes against them. Superficial social changes such as the end of the Inquisition, the elimination of legal discrimination on the basis of race, and the abolition of titles of nobility did occur. But independence left the existing economic and social structures intact. This was not surprising, for the creole elite that headed the movement had no intention of transforming the existing order. They sought to replace the *peninsulares* in the seats of power and to break the monopoly of trade held by Spain, not to change the labor and land systems. As producers of raw materials and foodstuffs for sale in the markets of Europe and North America, the plantation owners' interests required the maintenance of the system of great estates worked by a semiservile native population. No agrarian reform accompanied independence. The plantations abandoned by or confiscated from the loyalist Spaniards were often appropriated by the new creole aristocracy.

Central Americans had avoided a war with Mexico or with Spain in becoming independent. They could not avoid forever the pressures for social change that had been building in the final years of the colonial era. In the decades after independence, Central Americans should have engaged in the difficult process of nation building. Instead, they found themselves in a series of bitter civil wars that left the new governments impoverished and established a pattern of instability that has continued to the present.

Conservatives vs. Liberals: Two Ideals in Search of Reality

There is no better introduction to the confusing civil wars of the early years of independence in Latin America than this dialogue from *One Hundred Years of Solitude,* the epic novel of the Colombian novelist, Gabriel García Márquez:

> On one occasion on the eve of the elections, Don Apolinar Moscote returned from one of his frequent trips worried about the political situation in the country. The Liberals were determined to go to war. Since Aureliano at that time had very confused notions about the difference between Conservatives and Liberals, his father-in-law gave him some schematic lessons. The Liberals, he said, were Freemasons, bad people, wanting to hang priests, to institute civil marriage and divorce, to recognize the rights of illegitimate children as equal to those of legitimate ones, and to cut the country up into a federal system that would take power away from the supreme authority. The Conservatives, on the other hand, who had received their power directly from God, proposed the establishment of public order and family morality. They were the defenders of the faith of Christ, of the principle of authority, and were not prepared to permit the country to be broken down into autonomous entities. Because of his humanitarian feelings, Aureliano sympathized with the Liberal attitude with respect to the rights of natural children, but in any case, he could not understand how people arrived at the extreme of waging war over things that could not be touched with the hand.

>   *   *   *

> The elections took place without incident. At eight o'clock on Sunday morning, a wooden ballot box was set up in the square, which was watched over by the six soldiers. The voting was absolutely free, as Aureliano himself was able to attest since he spent almost the entire day with his father-in-law seeing that no one voted more than once. At four in the afternoon a roll of drums in the square announced the closing of the polls and Don Apolinar Moscote sealed the ballot box with a label crossed by his signature. That night, while he played dominoes with Aureliano, he ordered the sergeant to break the seal in order to count the votes. There were almost as many red ballots as blue, but the sergeant left only ten red ones and made up the difference with blue ones. Then they sealed the box again with a new label and the first thing on the following day it was taken to the capital of the province. "The Liberals will go to war," Aureliano said. Don Apolinar concentrated on his domino pieces. "If you're saying that because of the switch in ballots, they won't," he said. "We left a few red ones in so there won't be any complaints." Aureliano understood the disadvantages of being in the opposition. "If I were a Liberal," he said, "I'd go to war because of those ballots." His father-in-law looked at him over his glasses.
> "Come now, Aurelito," he said, "if you were a Liberal, even though you're my son-in-law, you wouldn't have seen the switching of the ballots."

Colonel Aureliano Buendía, having learned these lessons about the realities of power, goes on to fight and lose thirty-two wars between the Liberals and Conservatives. Leaders change sides, betray their principles, and rejoin once-spurned colleagues in García Márquez's masterpiece until it seems that political ideology serves as no more than a pretext for ritualistic warfare, a kind of Latin American version of the Hatfields and McCoys. Yet in almost all Latin American countries, and especially in Central America, the decades after independence were a time of partisan battles between Liberals and Conservatives.

In a sense, the way in which Central America became independent produced the period of civil wars. At its end, the Spanish imperial system was clearly not working well for either the colonizers or the colonized. Yet, instead of replacing it, independence movements in Central America attempted to preserve the essence of the old system while channeling benefits that used to go to the Spaniards to the newly dominant creole elite. Divisions within that elite and between the elite and the other classes were not reconciled as they might have been in a national struggle for independence. Rather, they were postponed, to be fought out when Central Americans had to decide what kind of independence they were to have. Should the new states preserve the traditional way of life, modifying and adapting the colonial heritage to changing circumstances, as Conservatives argued? Or should Central America cast off the burden of the Iberian heritage and embrace republican innovations from France, England, and the United States? Basic and provocative issues were at stake. What should be the relationship of the Catholic Church to the state in independent Central America? Should there be a strong central government as Conservatives wanted or a federation with weak central powers? Free trade, the Liberals argued, would lead to great advances for the Central American economies. Conservatives countered, correctly as it turned out, that unrestricted trade would cripple local industry and merchants who had long operated behind protective trade barriers.

Liberals, in particular, were attracted to the vision of Central America described by Simón Bolívar, the liberator of South America, as early as 1815:

The States of the Isthmus from Panama to Guatemala will perhaps form a confederation. This magnificent location between the two great oceans could in time become the emporium of the world. Its canals will shorten the distances throughout the world, strengthen commercial ties with Europe, America, and Asia, and bring that happy region tribute from the four quarters of the globe. Perhaps some day the capital of the world may be located there, just as Constantine claimed Byzantium as the capital of the ancient world.

The apparent success of England's former colonies in North America influenced political debates in Central America. Liberals argued that a confederation of the Central American states based on the North American model and constitution would guarantee Bolívar's vision of a glorious future for the region. Conservatives wanted a unitary system as had existed in colonial times. Liberals, although strongly Catholic in their personal beliefs, wanted to abolish church privileges (called *fueros*) and confiscate religious wealth. Conservatives upheld the religious and educational monopoly of the Roman Catholic Church and supported the *fueros* of the church and the military. Each side launched into civil war to press its case when excluded from power and ruthlessly suppressed its opponents when in power. Although fighting bitterly for the most high-minded political principles, each side used quite similar authoritarian methods to maintain itself in power. The conditions of war put a premium on military prowess rather than on statesmanship and ushered in the strongman on horseback, or *caudillo*, who through charisma, manipulation of the masses, or both succeeded for a time in enforcing order.

Divisions along ideological lines were reinforced by regional differences as the United Provinces began to fly apart. Rule by one element of the Liberal or Conservative faction in the capital of the federation would be opposed by their counterparts in some outlying state. By the mid-1840s, the combination of war and economic decline had put an end to Bolívar's dream of a united federation of Central American states. Unity would be an aspiration of future Central American leaders down to the present, but an unrealizable one.

It is hard to imagine a worse beginning for a newly independent region than that experienced by Central America in the thirty years after independence. Liberals and Conservatives held mutually exclusive visions of how Central American society should be organized. Although the Liberals carried the banner of change and progress, their ideals rarely coincided with Central American realities. Their free-trade policies destroyed native industry. The breakup of lands held by the Catholic Church was designed, Liberals argued, to improve the efficiency of agriculture and end the dominance of rural areas by the few. It resulted in an even tighter concentration of land (in the Liberal elite's hands, of course) and the elimination of many traditional holdings of Indian groups. In their desperation to counter Conservative policies and influence, the Liberals adopted highly authoritarian measures that violated many of their republican principles.

Neither Liberals nor Conservatives ever developed a vision of society that included all groups and classes. Their struggles ultimately became disputes among different sectors of a privileged elite for the right to continue to benefit from the exploitation of the many. Although Liberals and Conservatives often dominated politics in some of the Central American countries for long periods, neither side achieved complete success for its ideas or programs. Perhaps it would have been better for Central America in the long run to have seen the triumph of any one plan for the future, either Liberal or Conservative. Instead, the two sides wore each other down to a state of mutual exhaustion (and the financial bankruptcy of many governments).

In the absence of a final victory, that peculiar amalgam that strikes all visitors to Latin America was created. In what has been called Latin America's "living museum," ideas from all ages and ideologies coexist, none dominant, none replacing the other, none providing a coherent model to be followed. This is the special fascination of Latin America, but also its greatest weakness. The decades after independence in Central America witnessed much revolt but no revolution, no dramatic shift from old ideas and structures to new. Without a vision of the future, Central America soon reverted to its past of internal weakness and dependence on the new outside powers who were to replace Spain: first England and then the United States.

From Colony to Independence to Neocolony

Another passage from *One Hundred Years of Solitude* best describes much of Latin America's perception of the United States:

The gringos, who later on brought their languid wives in muslin dresses and large veiled hats, built a separate town across the railroad tracks with streets lined with palm trees, houses with screened windows, small white tables on the terraces, and fans mounted on the ceilings, and extensive blue lawns with peacocks and quails. The section was surrounded by a metal fence topped with a band of electrified chicken wire which during the cool summer mornings would be black with roasted swallows. No one knew yet what they were after, or whether they were actually nothing but philanthropists, and they had already caused a colossal disturbance, much more than that of the old gypsies, but less transitory and understandable. Endowed with means that had been reserved for Divine Providence in former times, they changed the pattern of the rains, accelerated the cycle of harvest, and moved the river from where it had always been and put it with its white stones and icy currents on the other side of the town, behind the cemetery. . . .

"Look at the mess we've got ourselves into," Colonel Aureliano Buendía said at that time, "just because we invited a gringo[2] to eat some bananas."

There are probably as many stories about the origin of the word *gringo* to refer to English-speaking foreigners in Latin America as there are Latin Americans. Some say it came from the soldiers' marching song during an invasion of Mexico when they sang "Green grow the lilacs," as they paraded in the capital. Others contend that the soldiers' green uniforms inspired the term. But all versions of its origin agree that it was coined to express popular hatred for the strange and arrogant northerners whom the Latin Americans and particularly the Central Americans found increasingly in their midst in the last half of the nineteenth century.

Most North Americans,[3] who are innocent of the deeds that promoted this hostility and may be ignorant of the history of their country's relations with Central America, understandably respond defensively to popular attitudes toward the "Colossus of the North," as the United States is unaffectionately known. They would find the unflattering portrait of the *gringos* painted by García Márquez to be unfair and overdrawn and be amused that the Latins viewed Yankee ingenuity as "means that had been reserved for Divine Providence in former times." These attitudes are, however, an essential part of Central America's history and are basic to understanding United States–Central American relations today.

It is perhaps easier to understand the sensitive nature of United States–Central American relations if one remembers that the Central Americans thought, naively as it turned out, that their independence would produce the kinds of advances that they had witnessed after the independence of North America. It was doubly hard to accept their own failures when they saw a country they had admired and, in some cases, tried to imitate, advancing beyond them and, ultimately, becoming a new imperial power.

Central America has always been an object of special attention for the United States. As a weak naval power and a relatively poor country, the United States did not provide much assistance to the independence movements in Latin America. From 1819 to 1821, a critical juncture for the independence movement, the United States was involved in delicate negotiations with Spain for the purchase of Florida and steered clear of any challenge to Spanish prerogatives in the region. But in one of its first major foreign policy initiatives, the United States placed itself on the side of independence, once achieved, in Latin America. On December 2, 1823, President James Monroe declared that, as a matter of principle, "the American continents, by the free and independent condition they have assumed and maintain, are henceforth not to be considered subjects for future colonization by any European powers. . . . We should consider any attempt on their [the European powers'] part to extend their system to any portion of this hemisphere as dangerous to our peace and safety." For its part, the United States pledged not to interfere with existing colonies nor to "meddle" in European affairs.

This Monroe Doctrine, as it was called, was largely ineffective for most of the nineteenth century, as the United States had neither the resources nor the determination to carry it out. But Great Britain, which did have a powerful fleet and a virtual monopoly of trade in the area, had an interest in blocking other European competitors. Although no formal colonies were reestablished, British and French gunboats regularly bombarded or blockaded Latin American ports to force payment of debts or reparations, without any response on the part of the United States.

Despite the high-minded statements about preserving Latin American independence, one can fairly describe the Monroe Doctrine as a way to close off Latin America to "outside" powers, while leaving the area open to intervention by the United States. This intervention was not only through trade, but included the landing of troops in the Falkland/Malvinas Islands, Argentina, and Peru during the 1830s; in Argentina, Nicaragua, Uruguay, Panama,

Paraguay, and Mexico during the 1850s; and in Panama, Uruguay, Mexico, and Colombia during the 1860s. Many Latin Americans began to worry about the intentions of the United States after the maneuvers to separate Texas from Mexico and eventually annex it, and the "trumped up war," as the young Abraham Lincoln called it, that appropriated the territories of Arizona, New Mexico, and California from Mexico in 1846–1847. Barely a half century old, the United States had successfully waged a war of territorial acquisition against Mexico, its closest Latin neighbor. It was only following, editorial writers of the day argued, its Manifest Destiny.[4]

In Central America, the mid-1800s were the age of the filibuster, or independent soldier of fortune. None would be more picturesque than William Walker, the "grey-eyed man of destiny." A historical marker in Memphis, Tennessee, tells the essential facts of his life: "Born May 8, 1824. In early life he was a doctor, lawyer, and journalist. He invaded Mexico in 1853 with 46 men and proclaimed himself President, Republic of Lower California. Led force into Nicaragua in 1855; was elected its President in 1856. In attempt to wage war on Honduras was captured and executed September 12, 1860."

Central American politics had become so out of control that adventurers like Walker with a few dozen men could tip the balance between Conservatives and Liberals and were often invited to do so by one side or the other. The interventionist designs of the United States and other powers complicated the politics of Central America in tragic ways, but they only took advantage of the failure of Central America's leaders to develop strong and effective political and economic systems that would discourage outside meddling.

The Liberals came to dominate most Central American countries in the last third of the nineteenth century. Their earlier concern for political freedom had now been supplanted by a preoccupation with material progress. New constitutions paid lip service to the republican principles of earlier Liberals, but in fact provided for centralized, executive-dominated governments with the military as the real arbiter of public affairs. In the ultimate irony, the triumph of Liberalism would be known as the Age of the Dictatorships.

In the continuing Central American fascination with importing ideas as well as luxury goods from Europe, the Liberals promoted the ideal of positivism, or the belief that science should rule the conduct of society. The idea of applying Darwin's theory of evolution to the social order prompted a concern with the "survival of the fittest" in Central America. The "fit" were, not unexpectedly, the more white and European elements in society. These elements were to be encouraged through domestic economic policies that would reward the aggressive and ambitious. Immigration laws were drawn up to increase the "fitness" of the Central American labor force by attracting a European working class. Instead, a small group of foreign entrepreneurs entered the region and became an arrogant class of merchants and planters.

With the demise or replacement of other export products, the Central American economies became increasingly focused on the production of coffee. Central America's rich volcanic soil and tropical climate gave many countries in the region a comparative advantage in coffee production. Legislation favoring export groups and the entrance of foreign capital increased the flow of raw materials out of the countries and augmented a dependence on foreign markets and capital. The explosion of demand for coffee created fortunes for the lucky few in Central America, but also led to the dangerous boom-and-bust cycles that overdependence on a single export commodity can produce. In their drive for economic prosperity, the Liberals had taken the quick route of reliance on the production of export commodities. They did not learn the lesson being taught in the more advanced countries of the period, that general economic improvement depended on the growth of a larger internal market and a rise in the level of daily wages.

With the ascendancy of the Liberals, one landed oligarchy had given way to another dedicated to a variation on the same traditional values. The new elites shared the advantages of modern civilization with foreign investors but not with the majority of their compatriots. As the preeminent historian of the region has concluded,

> The oligarchies had turned over control of their countries in large measure to foreign planters, merchants, financiers, diplomats, and, in the case of Nicaragua at least, even to foreign armed forces.

> . . . [The new Liberal oligarchy], based principally on producing and selling coffee to the wealthy nations, had political control, but it was a control that depended upon and had to be shared with the foreign interests, which increasingly came to be typified by the great banana company.[5]

Sam the Banana Man

There is perhaps no better symbol of the best and the worst of U.S. relations with Central America than the United Fruit Company (UFCO). Known as the "octopus" by its critics, for its ability to penetrate its business tentacles into every aspect of Central American politics and economics, UFCO was a dominant factor in many Central American countries for decades.

The history of United Fruit begins in 1870 when Captain Lorenzo Dow Baker of Wellfleet, Massachusetts, landed his schooner *Telegraph* in Jamaica and noticed the popularity of bananas in local markets. With the fruit largely unknown in the United States, Baker bought some green bananas and sold them eleven days later to curious vendors in Jersey City for a handsome profit.

Soon Baker, together with other investors, had established a regular trade in bananas between his home port of Boston and Jamaica, Cuba, and Santo Domingo. This Boston Fruit Company succeeded so well that the search began for new sources of supply that could produce bananas on a more sustained basis. That source was found in the person of Minor Keith, a Brooklyn-born entrepeneur who had been building railroads in Central America and exporting bananas to New Orleans and other ports to improve his cash flow. A deal was struck, and on March 13, 1899, Boston Fruit and Keith's enterprises became the United Fruit Company.

UFCO began with considerable assets, including 112 miles of railroad in Central America and 212,394 acres of land scattered throughout the Caribbean and Central America. Following a great tradition for foreign investors in Central America, UFCO became heavily involved in local politics, obtaining concessions to vast quantities of land and to monopolies of trade and transport that local corrupt rulers were only too happy to concede for the right price.

Among the shrewdest operators in this environment was Samuel Zemurray, the son of Russian peasants who became a powerful competitor of UFCO in Guatemala and Honduras until he was bought out and eventually named managing director of the entire corporation. *Bitter Fruit*, Schlesinger and Kinzer's story of the involvement of UFCO in Guatemala's politics, describes Zemurray's entry into Central America:

In 1905, Zemurray went to Honduras, then as now a major banana producer. His plan was to buy land, build a railroad to the coast and strike a bargain with local authorities that would grant him protection against tax increases and permission to import building materials without paying duty. He was horrified to learn that Honduran President Miguel Davila, looking for money to bail his country out of its chronic financial morass, was already in negotiation with a New York bank. In exchange for a loan, the New Yorkers insisted on naming their own agent to control Davila's national treasury—a common arrangement in those days.

Zemurray realized that no New York banker would grant him the one-sided concessions he was seeking, so he made a deal with one of Davila's enemies, a former Honduran leader named Manuel Bonilla, who was living in exile in the United States. Zemurray bought Bonilla a surplus navy ship, the *Hornet,* a case of rifles, a machine gun and a quantity of ammunition. He personally ferried Bonilla out of New Orleans harbor, slipping past Secret Service boats trying to prevent such expeditions, and sent the adventurers on their way. Within weeks, Honduras had had yet another revolution. When the dust cleared, Manuel Bonilla was President and "Sam the Banana Man" Zemurray was holding an agreement granting him every concession he sought.[6]

In some eyes, UFCO was a benevolent and paternal force in Central America. Its workers toiled under better conditions than most other farm laborers. Housing and medical facilities were built and schools provided for the children of workers. Some argued that Central Americans had not had the initiative nor the foresight to see their underdeveloped tropical lowlands as the site for a productive specialization in bananas.

But from the Central American viewpoint, the growth of the banana trade had its liabilities as well. The export orientation of the Central American economies, where they exported raw materials and imported finished goods, was maintained and reinforced, as was the social structure that benefited the few at the expense of the many. Although foreigners had been important in the coffee industry, bananas were the business almost exclusively of the *gringos.* The suspicion would always remain, and was often justified, that corrupt leaders had sold out the national patrimony at a cheap price. UFCO did not invent unsavory politics in Central America. But it contributed to them by engaging in unscrupulous business practices that had been banished in its home country. National pride was injured further by the racial policies of the company's mostly southern overseers, who required that "all persons of color . . . give right of way to whites and remove their hats while talking to them." This situation of poor countries dependent on outside markets, marked by corrupt politics and *yanqui* domination, led to the coining of the term *banana republic*.

The Roosevelt That Central Americans Don't Like

All that this country desires is to see the neighboring countries stable, orderly, and prosperous. Any country whose people conduct themselves well can count upon our hearty friendship. If a nation shows that it knows how to act with reasonable efficiency and decency in social and political matters, if it keeps order and pays its obligations, it need fear no interference from the United States. Chronic wrongdoing, or an impotence which results in a general loosening of the ties of civilized society, may in America, as elsewhere, ultimately require intervention by some civilized nation, and in the Western Hemisphere the adherence of the United States to the Monroe Doctrine may force the United States, however reluctantly, in flagrant cases of such wrongdoing or impotence, to the exercise of an international police power.

—The Roosevelt Corollary to the Monroe Doctrine, 1904.

The symbolic date marking the ascendancy of U.S. influence over the Spanish and British in Latin America is probably April 20, 1898, when the U.S. Congress ordered Spain to relinquish her authority and government in the island of Cuba, an act that led to the Spanish-American War and brought Theodore Roosevelt to public attention as one of the "Rough Riders" who stormed San Juan Hill. The loss of her final colony in the Americas produced a probing reexamination by Spanish intellectuals. But Spain's decline had been evident for more than a century, and it was really the British who had constituted the competition to U.S. influence in the region. With the dawn of the twentieth century, British and other European trade with and investments in Latin America began to decline and those of the United States dramatically increased, establishing a pattern that endured for the next sixty years. The "Colossus of the North" would be the dominant power in Latin America for most of the twentieth century.

The initial years after the Spanish-American War were a period that is almost universally denounced by Latin Americans. Phrases used by North Americans to characterize the period—the Big Stick, Gunboat Diplomacy, Dollar Diplomacy—give some flavor of the attitudes prevailing at that time.

The U.S. self-image portrays its relations with Latin America as, in large part, differing from those between great powers and weak ones because of the unique benevolence of U.S. policies. Yet for even the staunchest defenders of the good intentions of the United States in Latin America, the first third of the twentieth century represents a low point for U.S. policy.

Two examples of U.S. relations with the region during that period that are relevant to today's problems are the treatment of Cuba after the Spanish-American War and the building of the Panama Canal.

In the case of Cuba, questions about the good intentions of the United States in backing the Cuban struggle for independence were raised when the Platt Amendment was incorporated into the Cuban constitution in the early twentieth century. The amendment, named for the chairman of the Senate Foreign Relations Committee, dictated a series of terms to Cuba that severely limited her independence, until the amendment was withdrawn in 1934. Under the amendment Cuba was required to sell or lease lands to the United States for coaling or naval stations; her power to make treaties and her capacity to contract debts were limited; and the United States was given the right to intervene when it determined that Cuban independence was threatened or that law and order were not being maintained. In addition, the United States received the right to occupy a part of the island's territory, Guantánamo, in perpetuity. The Platt Amendment became a rallying cry for Cuban nationalists.

The building of the Panama Canal profoundly affected the future of Central America. From the time of Simón Bolívar, Latin Americans had speculated about the feasibility of a canal across the isthmus that would make the region, in Bolívar's words, "the capital of the world." Between 1878 and 1890, Ferdinand de Lesseps, the Frenchman who had constructed the Suez Canal, attempted to duplicate his feat across Panama, then a province of Colombia. Devastating tropical diseases and overwhelming engineering problems finally forced him to abandon the project, but the dream lived on.

Initial U.S. interest in a canal had centered on Nicaragua, and studies recommended that route as preferable. But the holders of the original French concession were desperate to recoup their losses on de Lesseps' earlier failure and lobbied the U.S. Congress hard to negotiate an agreement with the French canal company and the Colombian government. One clever ploy designed to discredit the alternate route through Nicaragua was to distribute postage stamps that pictured a "typical" Nicaraguan landscape: a jungle dominated by an active volcano. Clearly, it was argued, canals and volcanos do not mix. The promoters of the Panama route were also not above bribing members of the Republican party to switch their vote away from support for the Nicaraguan route.

Negotiations with the Colombian government over the canal during 1903 proved difficult. An initial treaty signed by the Colombian ambassador in Washington was rejected by the government in Bogotá. Colombia was at this time experiencing another of its periodic domestic upheavals and it would be difficult to characterize the government in power as representative. But there does seem to have been widespread public resentment of the U.S. terms of a $10 million, ninety-nine year lease and annual payments of $250,000. Roosevelt grew impatient and wrote at the time, "I do not think the Bogotá lot of jack rabbits should be allowed permanently to bar one of the future highways of civilization."

The solution to the difficulties with the Colombians lay in the long tradition of rebelliousness displayed by the province of Panama itself. The United States had, in fact, helped to put down earlier uprisings against the Colombians in the province. Now the United States permitted Phillipe Bunau-Varilla, chief engineer of the de Lesseps project and an organizer of the new company holding rights to the canal concession, to instigate, finance, and direct a revolt by the Panamanians. With the help of the U.S. Navy and bribes paid to the Colombian officers who were supposed to crush the rebellion, Panama won its independence in 1903.

In a decision they were later to regret, the Panamanians entrusted negotiations over a canal concession to the same Bunau-Varilla. Desperate to work out an agreement before his company's rights to the concession expired, he agreed to a treaty that would pay the same amount that had been offered to Colombia, $10 million and an annual $250,000 payment, but for the *perpetual* use, occupation, and control of a ten-mile-wide canal zone through Panama in which the United States would exercise rights "as if it were sovereign of the territory." The new Panamanian government protested the terms of the treaty, but ultimately accepted it, fearing that the United States might either seize the canal with no compensation or build one in Nicaragua instead.

While Teddy Roosevelt was to proudly proclaim, "I took the canal," relations between Panama and the United States remained difficult for years, until a new treaty was negotiated in the late 1970s that will eventually turn control of the canal over to Panama by the twenty-first century. A U.S. Senator seemed to recapture the spirit of Teddy Roosevelt's approach to Central America during debate of the 1977 treaty when he argued against turning the canal over to Panama because "we stole it fair and square."

In arguing against the Panama Canal treaties in 1976, soon-to-be-President Ronald Reagan often pointed out the engineering and health-care marvel that the United States had wrought in constructing the canal on time and on budget and in defeating the tropical diseases that had decimated the ranks of workers on previous construction projects in the jungle. There is no question that the canal, with its intricate system of locks and channels, constituted a tremendous human achievement in its day and does even now. The United States did what others had failed to do and opened a passage to trade that benefited not only the United States, but the rest of the world.

These arguments missed the point, however, that for most Panamanians the method by which the Canal Zone was obtained and the maintenance of a foreign presence and lifestyle within their borders constituted an affront to their national dignity. Even fellow conservatives such as William F. Buckley, Jr., argued against Mr. Reagan that reaching an agreement with Panama over the canal was more likely to preserve its status as a free waterway open to the world and to retain Panama as a friendly neighbor of the United States.

Theodore Roosevelt's high-handed methods for obtaining the canal took advantage of Central America's inability to establish stable and representative governments and followed a pattern that had been established even before the United States became a major actor in the region. His actions ushered in a period of nearly thirty years in which the United States would be more actively involved in the day-to-day affairs of Central America than at any other time—until the present. That active involvement would mean that in the future, the United States was not only taking advantage of Central America's weaknesses, but would be held partially responsible for promoting and perpetuating them.

"After Fifty Years, Sandino Lives Again"

Traveling around Nicaragua in 1984 a visitor encountered numerous silhouettes of a man dressed in a cowboy hat with trousers tucked in knee-high boots. The slogan below the silhouette said it all, *A 50 Años, Sandino Vive,* (After Fifty Years, Sandino Lives Again). The figure is that of Augusto Sandino, who became a hero for many Nicaraguans by fighting and eluding U.S. Marines during the nearly twenty-year occupation of Nicaragua by the United States after 1912. His struggle and death in 1934 inspired a revolution that preoccupies the United States today because of the revolution's ties to Cuba and the Soviet Union. The story of Sandino and of U.S. involvement in Nicaragua in the first third of the twentieth century is a rather extreme example of U.S.–Central American relations, but an illustrative one.

The Panama Canal was the most visible symbol of increasing U.S. economic and political involvement in Central American affairs. The increased stake of the United States in the region heightened its sensitivity to the "chronic wrongdoing" that had afflicted Central American politics since independence and encouraged the United States to exercise the "international police power" of which Roosevelt had spoken in his famous corollary. The occasion of "chronic wrongdoing" in Nicaragua was a rather typical squabble between Conservatives who were out of power in Nicaragua and the Liberals who had another in their series of dictators in the presidency. Liberal President Zelaya had alienated some of his Conservative countrymen with attacks on the church and had upset foreign businessmen by increasing taxes. When a revolt by Conservatives, assisted financially by North American and other foreign interests, broke out in 1909 and led to the death of two U.S. citizens who were fighting with the rebels, the United States entered the civil war on the side of the Conservatives. With U.S. military help, the Conservatives gained power and ultimately installed as president Adolfo Díaz, a former employee of a U.S. mining concession in Nicaragua. At one point some 2,000 U.S. Marines occupied strategic positions in Nicaragua to maintain Díaz and the Conservatives in power. A treaty conferring a virtual protectorate status on Nicaragua was signed, and a smaller contingent of Marines remained from 1912 until 1925, supervising elections and discouraging Liberal challenges to the Conservatives. Following the election of a Conservative president in 1925, the Marines withdrew, but new rebellions broke out almost immediately.

Bitter warfare between the Liberals and Conservatives, involving a growing number of U.S. troops and aircraft, continued for three years until a Liberal general agreed to a truce. Feeling the Liberal cause had been betrayed, Augusto Cesar Sandino, the son of a small landholder and an Indian peasant, chose to fight on. He and his ragged troops were defeated in battle after battle until they adopted the hit-and-run tactics we know today as guerrilla warfare. He eluded the U.S. Marines and the Nicaraguan National Guard, which the United States was training to take over military supervision of the country. Only the election, in 1932, of a Liberal president who had campaigned on a platform of U.S. withdrawal could persuade Sandino to give up his fight against the "Yankee imperialists." In January 1933 the last U.S. troops left Nicaragua. But long-term damage had been done. Anastasio Somoza, the bilingual head of the National Guard and lover of the U.S. ambassador's wife, had Sandino assassinated as he was leaving the National Palace on the night of February 21, 1934. By 1936, Somoza had removed the elected Liberal president and installed himself as the head of a political dynasty that ruled Nicaragua for the next forty years.

Although denounced by the United States as a bandit, Sandino was in the eyes of many a nationalist fed up with the failures of the ruling political elites and their willingness to invite foreign intervention to bolster the position of one side or the other. In death he became a hero, and thirty years later, the inspiration to young Nicaraguans who would take up arms against the son of the original Somoza. In 1979 the Sandinista National Liberation Front defeated Somoza and made Sandino live again after fifty years. The Sandinista anthem, in the spirit of Sandino, denounces the Yankee as the "enemy of humanity."

The Old System Begins to Break Down

The intervention of the United States in Nicaragua was more far-reaching than those in other Central American countries, but it reflected an increasing preoccupation on the part of the United States with the region. Unfortunately for the United States, this heightened concern for stability in the area coincided with a period of great change in the domestic politics of Central America. New social groups emerged to challenge the traditional elites for a share of power, and provocative ideas such as nationalism and socialism made themselves felt in intellectual circles. At a time when many Central Americans were desperate for change to better their lives, U.S. policy often came to be equated with support for the status quo. This was a legacy that has burdened U.S. policies in the region until the present.

The efforts of the Liberals to modernize and develop their societies in the late nineteenth and early twentieth centuries had not achieved the kind of general prosperity and progress that had been hoped for. Rather, certain sectors of the economy and society, the better-off and urban dwellers, had advanced while the rural countryside had languished in a poverty dominated by the values and institutions of a century before. Rural inhabitants were lured to the cities by the often unfulfilled promise of employment and economic advancement, and they formed pockets of poverty that would eventually become huge slums around the capitals and other large cities. Achievements in the control of epidemic diseases and other improvements in medical care led to a drop in infant mortality rates and a dramatic increase in the population.

In these expanding cities, a much more significant middle class began to emerge. But the middle class was not dominant in most Central American countries as it was in the United States. Weak and dependent, the Central American middle class aped their upper-class compatriots, who set the tone for society and continued to monopolize political life. The refusal of the traditional elites to make way for the middle class and other new groups in the political arena eventually led to revolutionary turmoil. Only in Costa Rica, always an exception to the Central American rule, was such turmoil avoided.

Insignificant numerically but important because of their concentration in the centers of political power, workers organized themselves into unions that often had a radical cast of Marxism or socialism. Examples and pressure from outside the region led to legislation that, formally at least, recognized minimum labor rights such as the forty-eight hour week, overtime pay, worker's compensation, and so on.

The emphasis of the Liberals on education had increased the impact of university students and intellectuals on the political system. The upper class still sent its children abroad to be educated, but national universities in Central America became middle-class institutions and accelerated the aspirations of this group. This educated elite experimented with a range of ideologies from communism to fascism, but all focused increasingly on the need for greater nationalism. Conscious of their status as underdeveloped nations, Central Americans' nationalism was often rooted in resentment, fear, frustration, and a sense of inferiority. It was frequently violent and angry, and it had a strong impact on the rest of the population.

Costa Rica, Always the Exception

The generalizations that have been made about Central America throughout this chapter cannot do justice to the richness and complexity of the individual countries' histories. But the story of Costa Rica's development is especially different from that of the rest of Central America.

In the late 1980s, Costa Rica is far from a paradise and has severe economic and social strains. But while the recent history of much of the rest of the region is a story of death, destruction, and dictatorship, Costa Rica has been a functioning democracy that abolished a standing army and instituted far-reaching social reforms more than forty years ago.

Just as the origins of many of the rest of Central America's problems lie in history, so too are the reasons for Costa Rica's relative success found in her past. Despite her name, Rich Coast, the early Spanish explorers found little of the mineral wealth in Costa Rica that attracted them to other parts of Central America. Those Spaniards who decided to settle in what was to become Costa Rica fought fierce battles with the small indigenous population and virtually eliminated them. Without mines or a subservient labor force to work plantation-style agriculture, the early colonists set up small family farms similar to those found in North America. As a result, the tiny aristocratic elite that ruled the rest of Central America never developed as fully in Costa Rica. The slight economic importance of Costa Rica to Spain and its relative isolation meant that Hispanic institutions were never as strongly imposed on Costa Rica's small population as they were on those of the other Central American countries. The country's politics, therefore, were always more egalitarian and middle class than those prevailing in the rest of Central America. The elimination of the native population allowed Costa Rica to avoid the problems caused by racial mixing and color barriers. By 1925 the population was nearly 80 percent white with a small *mestizo* group (14 percent), a tiny black population concentrated on the coasts, and an Indian group of less than 1 percent.

There were clearly differences between rich and poor. But there also developed an agrarian middle sector—virtually unknown in the rest of Central America—based on family-sized farms that allowed a wider distribution of wealth. No landless subclass dominated the countryside. The agrarian middle sector and a relatively literate and democratically-oriented urban population placed checks on foreign domination of the economic life of the country. Costa Rica specialized in both coffee and bananas, as did the rest of Central America. But an elected leadership, more responsive to popular needs, made foreign participation in the economy more a partnership than a case of exploitation. The government levied taxes on UFCO's operations and required that railroads be constructed and other benefits bestowed on the state in return for concessions on banana lands.

When the Western capitalist economy collapsed in 1929 and desperation drove popular forces to consider radical alternatives such as communism and fascism, strong-arm dictators seized power in every Central American country except Costa Rica. Even in Costa Rica there were riots, worker uprisings, and suspension of constitutional guarantees. But unlike the other countries, Costa Rica produced political parties that promised reform and offered effective alternatives to communism or fascism as ways to resolve social conflict. In the rest of Central America, where powerful oligarchies feared the masses and where tiny middle classes had no control over the political system, right-wing dictatorships were the response to the political and economic crises of the 1930s.

Depression and Repression

Throughout Latin America, the decline of export markets and the fall in prices because of the world depression of the 1930s produced challenges to the traditional method of politics. This happened in Central America as well. The reaction of the traditional elites was to find a strong man who could hold the forces of change in check at least for a while. Whether it was General Jorge Ubico in Guatemala (1931–1944), General Maximiliano Hernández Martínez in El Salvador (1931–1944), Anastasio Somoza in Nicaragua (1936–1956), or Tiburcio Carías Andino in Honduras (1932–1949), the methods of power were strikingly similar: censorship of the press, exile or jail for the opposition, pervasive police control, special privileges for the prominent coffee producers, and generous treatment of the interests of foreign corporations.

The reaction against popular protest took monstrous proportions in some cases. In El Salvador a peasant uprising in January 1932 was led by Augusto Farabundo Martí, head of the fledgling Communist party. Several landlords were murdered, and the movement threatened to establish a collective-based government. The army defeated the poorly equipped band of Indian rebels and then began a systematic slaughter of the Indian population in the rebel region. Between 10,000 and 40,000 peasants died in the army's action. Today in El Salvador, one of the death squads is named in honor of General Hernández and his response to challenges from the left. The coalition of guerrilla groups, the Farabundo Martí Liberation Front (FMLN), takes its name from the fallen Communist leader.

Somoza's system of control in Nicaragua was perhaps the most sophisticated. Power was concentrated in his own hands and those of his political family. Opposition—particularly of the left—was ruthlessly repressed, but he was kept in power by more than the U.S.-trained National Guard. His emphasis on material progress— at least for the privileged few—helped to create the strongest and most durable family dynasty in Central American history. He and, after his assassination, his family controlled nearly every facet of

Nicaraguan economic life: land, industry, banking, transportation, and commerce. It was estimated that by 1970 they owned more than half the agricultural production of the republic and had vast financial resources invested in industry, mining, and commerce in and outside Nicaragua.

Somoza continued his earlier close association with the "Yankees" who had helped place him in power. He received increasing amounts of economic and military assistance and acknowledged the importance of the United States to his regime by locating the U.S. embassy virtually on the grounds of the presidential palace. As Franklin Roosevelt said of Somoza, "He's a son of a bitch, but he's ours."

Franklin Delano Roosevelt and the Good Neighbor Policy

The period of blatant intervention by the United States during the first third of the twentieth century eventually produced a strong reaction throughout Latin America. Repeatedly in inter-American conferences during the period, Latin American critics of U.S. policy in the region raised the issue of nonintervention in the internal and external affairs of the Latin American republics. An active participant in two earlier interventions by President Wilson in Mexico and Haiti, Roosevelt argued that a change was needed in U.S.–Latin American relations. While campaigning for governor of New York in 1928, he wrote an article for *Foreign Affairs* magazine that criticized U.S. interventions in the Caribbean region and demanded the renunciation "for all time" of "arbitrary intervention in the home affairs of our neighbors." As president, he pledged the United States to pursue the policy of a good neighbor in her international relations.

Roosevelt's good intentions were reinforced by the increasing problems in Europe during the 1930s. Several conflicts between nationalistic governments and U.S. businesses were resolved in Latin America's favor, most notably the nationalization of the oil industry in Mexico in 1938. As war clouds increased in Europe, Roosevelt became more concerned about the loyalty of the Mexican government than about the economic interests of the large corporations and forced accommodation on companies used to unquestioning defense of their prerogatives.

Critics of U.S. policy toward Latin America question the degree to which Roosevelt actually changed U.S. behavior toward the region. But in Central America the popular perception is that Roosevelt's Good Neighbor Policy was successful. The record of that success remains in the schools, hospitals, and roads named after the president or the first lady and in the positive response his memory evokes among the common people.

The War and Its Aftermath: Reform or Revolution?

The wartime partnership between the United States and Latin America lasted about as long as that between the United States and the Soviet Union. Scarcity produced by the war years was a boon to the export economies of Central America, but increased prosperity only caused greater discontent with the repressive dictatorships that had ruled much of Central America since the Great Depression. In rapid succession, the dictators of Guatemala (1944), El Salvador (1944), and Honduras (1948) were overthrown, and even Somoza in Nicaragua was forced to juggle a series of puppet presidents to maintain his grip on power.

New ideas about social change and economic development pervaded the postwar world. Diverse social groups such as university professors and students, government officials, small businessmen and urban artisans, and some elements of the professional military tentatively supported social reforms. These reforms included minimal social security legislation providing medical assistance and unemployment compensation, the right to unionize, and a labor code. In the economic sphere, there was agreement on the need for some state control of the banking and credit industries, plans for agricultural reform, and a policy of economic diversification. As regards politics, reinforcing constitutional, representative democracy and the principle of electoral politics—one, but not the only route to power in Central America—were priorities. Finally, taxation of the banana companies, as one of a series of nationalist measures, completed this basic reform program.

The relative success or failure of these reform programs depended on several factors. One was the ability of the dominant class to move against the reforms. The traditional elites saw any concession on reformist issues as opening the road to social revolution and, in the Cold War atmosphere that came to dominate the post-war period, they adopted an anticommunist ideology that branded as "red" even the most modest changes. As the case of Costa Rica illustrates, a second factor determining the possibilities for reform was the relative importance of the middle sectors and the opportunity they had to play a political role supportive of reform. A final factor was the prevailing international context and in particular the policy of the United States. As events in Guatemala in the 1950s demonstrated, the ability of the United States to distinguish between reform and revolution had profound implications for the future of reformist projects in Central America.

A Harvest of Bitter Fruit

From October 1944 to June 1954, Guatemala lived out a reformist drama. Depending on one's perspective, the U.S.-organized invasion that ended this social experiment in 1954 was either the first successful rebuff to communist designs on the hemisphere or a tragic misreading of the reformist impulse in Central America that would lead to the more troublesome conflicts of the 1980s in El Salvador and Nicaragua.

Ubico's long dictatorship finally ended in mid-1944. Elections in December brought Dr. Juan José Arévalo, an exiled educator and philosopher, to power. An intellectual and idealistic man, Dr. Arévalo promulgated a vague doctrine of "spiritual socialism," which seemed to offer the hope of change without committing the country to a revolutionary program. Elected by a broad front that won over 85 percent of the vote, Arévalo moved to implement a reformist program. His government established social security, founded a Native People's Institute for Guatemala's majority Indian population, and developed health programs, a labor code, and a state organization devoted to the promotion of economic development.

The fall of Ubico had brought back many political exiles who carried with them some of the Marxist and leftist ideas to which they had been exposed in exile. They, together with foreigners attracted to the possibility for social change, sought to develop a Marxist ideology among Guatemalan workers and political leaders.

The appeal of communism to Guatemalan workers was not surprising. No other domestic group sought to attract their allegiance. Ignorant of the international communist movement and of the political and economic theory it espoused, the average worker knew that he had been economically and socially exploited and oppressed and prohibited from organizing effectively to support his own interests. Communist intellectuals, foreign and Guatemalan, offered to the worker the possibility of advancement, while no one else seemed to care.

As the election of 1950 approached, the internal political situation began to polarize. The new pro-worker legislation and the proliferation of unions provoked conflicts with the important interests of the United Fruit Company and challenged the privileged position of the coffee producers. There were twenty-two military revolts during Arévalo's five years in the presidency. On occasion the government issued arms to workers to aid in the suppression of the military revolts.

The election of Colonel Jacobo Arbenz in 1950 began the countdown to the end of Guatemala's experiment. An agrarian reform law was passed in 1952 that affected all landowners with over 250 acres, especially United Fruit, which controlled about 550,000 acres on Guatemala's Atlantic and Pacific coasts. The expropriation of over 200,000 acres of uncultivated land held in reserve by United Fruit brought the confrontation to a head. The Guatemalan government offered $600,000 in bonds as compensation for the land, an amount based on UFCO's declared tax value. As was customary among foreign companies operating in Central America, UFCO undervalued its property for tax purposes and screamed in protest to the U.S. government when this understated value was used as the basis for compensation. The United States presented, on behalf of UFCO, a demand for over $16 million in compensation.

UFCO was well positioned in Washington during the Eisenhower administration. Secretary of State John Foster Dulles had done legal work for clients connected to UFCO, as had his brother, Allen Dulles, head of the CIA. John Moors Cabot, Assistant Secretary of State for Inter-American Affairs, had family holdings in UFCO, and his brother Thomas had served as president of the corporation in 1948. United Nations Ambassador Henry Cabot Lodge was also a stockholder and had defended UFCO's interests many times as the senator from Massachusetts.

For many in and outside Guatemala, the attack on United Fruit was proof positive that Guatemala was falling into communist hands. The CIA was authorized to mount operation *El Diablo* (The Devil) to remove Arbenz and the purported communist threat. A complex series of maneuvers ensued, involving the training of an exile army in Honduras led by two former Guatemalan officers opposed to the reforms, the obtaining of international support, CIA aerial bombings to intimidate Arbenz supporters, and the condemnation of an arms shipment from Czechoslovakia (the United States had previously blocked Guatemalan arms purchases from noncommunist countries). After losing the support of the military and refusing to call out the unions to battle the invaders, Arbenz resigned on June 27, 1954, seven days after the CIA army had entered Guatemalan territory. One of the first acts of the new leader of Guatemala, Castillo Armas, was to return the expropriated property to United Fruit.

The "lessons" of Guatemala were different for each of the parties involved. For the right in Guatemala and in the United States, a blow had been struck against the international communist conspiracy and a country "liberated" from communist rule in a way that Eastern Europe apparently could not be. Moderates thought the coup a tragic misreading of nationalist aspirations in Central America. A modest reform program—much less far-reaching than that promoted by the United States in El Salvador in the 1980s—had been branded as communism and basic changes that had a possibility of preventing a truly explosive situation had been rejected. The left drew the conclusion that no middle road was possible and that U.S. imperialism would oppose any reform in Latin America that threatened the interests of its large corporations. Ernesto "Che" Guevara, the Argentine revolutionary who later came to power with Fidel Castro in Cuba, watched the U.S.-engineered coup from a post in the Guatemalan agrarian reform institute. He viewed as key the betrayal of Arbenz by the traditional armed forces and eliminated the army as a threat to Cuba's revolution after 1959.

Since the 1950s, the specter of Soviet intervention in Latin America has haunted U.S. policy toward the region. Cynical Latin Americans, mindful of the Monroe Doctrine, have argued that the supposed communist threat was just the latest in a series of convenient pretexts that the United States used for maintaining its position of dominance. They have pointed out that the poverty, disease, and exploitation that the Central American elites have helped to create cannot be overcome by appeals to democratic slogans. Instead a frontal assault on the privileges and power that have been amassed in the hands of the few would be required. If the United States would not help to change this situation, weren't patriots justified in seeking help from outside powers who, for their own strategic reasons, were interested in seeing the status quo altered?

The Alliance That Lost Its Way

Perhaps the dilemma for U.S. policy in Central America was best presented by President John F. Kennedy who coined the axiom, "Those who make peaceful change impossible make violent change inevitable." Complacent about Central America for decades, the United States was unprepared to deal with the wave of social change that swept through the Third World in the postwar period. Central America's ruling groups were ready to resist change with every means at their disposal. When the inevitable confrontation came, which side would the United States choose?

The answer given by the handsome young president elected in 1960 was that the United States would prefer reformist democracies to right-wing dictators and left-wing revolutions. His proposal for an Alliance for Progress with Latin America was the most comprehensive aid program ever undertaken toward the region. Launched as a self-conscious response to the Cuban revolution of 1959, the Alliance held out the prospect of long-term economic development, social reform, and political democratization as alternatives to violent change. Its programs called upon Latin America's elites to take what were for them radical steps such as land reform, progressive tax legislation, and development projects aimed at the poorest sectors of the population.

But an Alliance that held great promise eventually lost its way. The program was suspect not only for the radical left, but also for the recalcitrant right. The meaningful reforms called for by the Alliance attacked the privileged positions of economic elites. They resisted measures squarely in the center of U.S. social and political values as steps on the road to socialism. The program had always had an important security component of military and police aid and training to protect reformist efforts from revolutionary attack. As Kennedy's beloved Green Berets went off to fight communism in Vietnam, the emphasis of the Alliance shifted from reform to security. By 1965 when Lyndon Johnson sent 20,000 marines into the Dominican Republic it was clear that the United States believed it could no longer risk social experimentation that might produce "another Cuba." In a tragic turn of events, one of the Alliance's enduring legacies was to have trained many of the military leaders who came to dominate Latin American politics in the 1960s and 1970s.

To the Contemporary Crisis

The decades of the 1960s and 1970s in Central America saw the continued emergence of new social groups and political actors. The middle class, historically a small minority in Central American politics, had grown larger and become more diverse. Its challenge to the traditional oligarchic structure forced the ruling elites to defend themselves by seeking new allies in the military and through anticommunist appeals to the United States. In some cases, the working class and the peasantry developed mass organizations that were also capable of confronting the traditional power structure. Explosive combinations were created when disaffected elements of the middle class, following the Cuban model, linked up with mass-based organizations of peasants or workers.

The military as an institution had changed dramatically over the course of the twentieth century. In the first third of the century, it developed into one of the few semimeritocratic institutions in Central America. The creation of military schools with entrance by examination opened a new route to social status for those from the lower middle class. Now the son of a poor schoolteacher, minor government official, or small shopowner could aspire to achieve real power, even the presidency of his country, and to appropriate through corruption the wealth that political power made possible.

The military ranks did not remain a monolith. They too were affected by the currents of social change swirling through society at large. Some elements, often the younger officers who saw their possibilities of advancement blocked by a top-heavy senior officer corps, forged links with progressive civilians and attempted to institute reforms to preempt more drastic revolutionary change. These progressive coups rarely endured, however, because of the unwillingness of the military to institutionalize reform through civilian and popularly based political structures.

The more common pattern was for the military to strike a deal with the old landholding oligarchies to defend their interests by force and repression. In return for their protection, the military were allowed to take a cut of the economic pie. This arrangement endured in many of the Central American countries for much of the 1960s and 1970s. But it began to break down under the pressure of economic shocks delivered to the region in the 1970s and the continued emergence of new challenges to the status quo.

A significant new actor on the Central American scene during the 1970s was a progressive Catholic Church. From Spanish colonial times on, the church had generally been viewed as an ally of the rich and powerful. Its response to the deprivation of most of its flock was to counsel patience and comfort in the consolation of a heavenly reward for those who had suffered in this life. Linked to the elite by interest as well as birthright, the Catholic Church had played, with rare exceptions, a role consistently supportive of the status quo.

In the 1960s and 1970s, new forces began to stir in the church. Inspired by the doctrines of renewal developed by the Second Vatican Council (1962–1965), many in the Latin American church sought to break the long-standing association of the Catholic Church with the interests of the powerful. First in Medellín, Colombia in 1968, and later in 1979 in Puebla, Mexico, Roman Catholic bishops of Latin America met to examine critically the role of the church in their societies. In these meetings, they condemned the institutionalized violence of the status quo and indicted those with "the greater share of wealth and power" who "jealously retain their privileges thus provoking 'explosive revolutions of despair.'" In dramatic statements, they took it upon themselves to defend the rights of the poor and oppressed and to encourage efforts by the poor to develop their own grassroots organizations. Criticizing both capitalism and communism, their pronouncements often seemed to support a kind of benign socialism that would recognize the communal nature of human beings while not violating basic rights of liberty and religious freedom. Some within the church spoke of the development of a "Christian Marxism" and a "theology of liberation." A few prominent priests went to the hills to join guerrilla struggles. In Nicaragua in the late 1970s, the church was a powerful force in helping to overthrow the Somoza dynasty. El Salvador's Archbishop Romero, before his assassination by the right in 1980, was also an eloquent critic of the power structure and a spokesperson for the poor and the politically repressed.

In the 1980s, reaction to these liberalizing trends in the church set in. More conservative bishops, who had always been uncomfortable with the idea of "liberation theology," reasserted the church hierarchy's prerogatives. The Polish Pope, John Paul II, who had direct experience with the conflicts between the church and a communist state, cautioned against too political a stance for priests. In Nicaragua, church authorities clashed with the Sandinista leadership and splits developed between the church hierarchy, increasingly opposed to the Sandinistas, and the so-called popular church of priests and nuns who worked with the poor and even occupied cabinet positions in the Sandinista government.

Despite these signs of internal turmoil, the church by the late 1980s was clearly not the conservative institution it had been only fifteen or twenty years before. Together with other changes in Central American society, the new Catholic Church was a powerful indicator that the old order would come under increasing attack.

That old order had in fact exhausted itself by the early 1960s. One of the surest signs of its demise was the increasing irrelevance of the old party labels of Liberal and Conservative. A proliferation of new parties and movements emerged over the course of the 1960s and 1970s, sometimes representing factions of the old parties, but often introducing new strains into the political mix. The new parties frequently drew their inspiration from Western Europe, not the United States. Examples included the Christian Democrats, who won the presidency of El Salvador in 1972 and 1984 and of Guatemala in 1985, and were also important in other Central American countries. They tried to combine the region's tradition of Catholicism with progressive social policies that were, nevertheless, staunchly anticommunist. Various Social Democratic tendencies emerged that were also anticommunist, but even more disposed than the Christian Democrats to promote state intervention in civil society. Anticommunist socialist parties developed, again inspired by European traditions. Each of these political formations was strengthened by regional and international links with similar parties in Latin America and in Europe.

On the right, various groupings developed that sought to defend traditional interests through the new methods of popular appeals and the ballot box. Among the more interesting experiments were attempts to imitate the Mexican single party state by dominating the political system while tolerating a feeble opposition.

Another group that entered Central American politics with a vengeance in the 1960s was leftist guerrillas. Largely inspired by the perceived success of armed struggle in Cuba, groups of students, intellectuals, and other disaffected members of the middle class took to the hills (or jungles) and attempted to recruit peasants to the cause of revolution. Some of these revolutionaries were moderates who had despaired of peaceful attempts to achieve social change. Others were members of socialist or communist parties who grew disillusioned with the willingness of their parties' leadership to work within the system.

Cuban-inspired guerrilla movements met with spectacular failures in most of Latin America and helped to precipitate, in some cases, the brutal authoritarian regimes of the 1960s and 1970s. In a pattern that would be repeated later in other Central American countries, the guerrillas had some success in that country where reformist approaches had been defeated: Guatemala. Guerrilla movements led by rebellious army officers began in Guatemala in the late 1950s and continued with intermittent success throughout the 1960s and 1970s. The guerrillas' actions produced the now classic response: death squads—semiofficial assassination teams operating above the law—and U.S. counterinsurgency advisers. After 1966, Guatemala unleashed a withering attack on the "forces of subversion." More than 30,000 people were tortured or assassinated. In the ferocious warfare, much of the moderate center as well as the left was eliminated. During the 1980s, when the guerrillas again began to make inroads in the Indian population, a savage war was mounted that adopted the old North American slogan, "The only good Indian is a dead Indian." Cut off from U.S. aid because of disputes over human rights abuses during the

Carter administration, Guatemala's military adopted tactics that probably violated all the conventions of modern warfare, but "pacified" the countryside once more.

In Nicaragua, guerrilla bands named for the fallen patriot Augusto Sandino began operations against the Somozas in the 1960s. They were largely unsuccessful until "Tachito" Somoza, son of the first dictator, scandalized even his supporters by misappropriating disaster relief aid for the devastating 1972 earthquake that virtually destroyed the capital, Managua. Castro's Cuba also played a role in the guerrillas' success by serving as a training base, by forging coalitions among the conflicting guerrilla groups, and by providing direct military assistance in the final decisive months. The Sandinistas came to power in 1979 at the head of a broad front of anti-Somoza opposition groups after a civil war that cost 40,000 lives.

The other site of relative success by the guerrillas was El Salvador. In 1979, another in a series of reformist military coups provoked a civil war that has taken an estimated 70,000 lives. Guerrillas, linked politically to democratic-minded politicians who had abandoned hope for peaceful reform, were able to occupy one-fourth of the national territory. However, government forces, with massive U.S. assistance, gradually forced a stalemate in the war.

The Soviet Union opposed Castro's armed struggle strategy for much of the 1960s and 1970s as risky and unproductive. It preferred to influence events through the conventional approach of pro-Moscow communist parties. If the Sandinistas' success has persuaded the Soviet Union of the correctness of Cuba's strategy, there is no clear indication of a change in the Soviet approach yet. Despite their commitments to Cuba and the unrelenting U.S. hostility to Nicaragua, the Soviet Union was by the late 1980s reducing its aid levels to Nicaragua and signaling its interest in Sandinista accommodation to regional negotiations. Trade and aid agreements and significant programs of cultural exchange, rather than support for revolutionary uprisings, marked Soviet policy in Latin America in the 1980s.

The Simmering Pot of Central America

The crisis now gripping Central America has multiple dimensions. One underlying cause of the escalation of conflict during the

1970s was the severe economic contraction that hit the Third World in general and especially the small Central American countries after the oil shocks of 1973 and 1979. Escalating oil costs and declining prices for Central America's exports impoverished the region and forced the countries to accumulate huge external debts to maintain prior standards of living.

The dream of Central America's reunification was reborn in the 1960s with the establishment of a Central American Common Market that promised to improve economic conditions by expanding the size of each country's potential market. Industrialization to substitute for imports was intended to diversify Central America away from its traditional dependence on exports of coffee, bananas, and cotton. Central America was following the advice given to most other developing countries that continued reliance on traditional exports would doom their economies to chronic poverty. Demand for coffee, bananas, or other tropical exports did not rise as quickly as incomes in the rich countries. To buy crucial imports, the Central American countries had to export larger and larger amounts of their products at the same or reduced prices. Import substitution, it was argued, would lessen costly imports and begin a process of industrialization that would allow the countries to produce new exports. The Common Market would complement this process by lowering tariff barriers between the countries and expanding the potential market size beyond each country's own relatively small population. Foreign aid, principally from the United States, and foreign investment added the necessary infusion of capital to launch the process.

The Common Market began auspiciously. Trade within the region multiplied sevenfold between 1961 and 1968. But over time, market forces tended to accentuate rather than lessen differences among the countries. Guatemala and El Salvador, the countries with greater population and lower salaries, benefited disproportionately from the Common Market, while Nicaragua, Costa Rica, and, especially, Honduras grew increasingly resentful of the effects of the market on their economies. The so-called Soccer War between El Salvador and Honduras in 1969, which began with violence at a soccer match and was fueled by the large number of Salvadoran immigrants in Honduras, made maintenance of the market more difficult. Honduras eventually withdrew from the market in 1971.

By the end of the 1970s, the alternative model of development offered by the Common Market appeared to have failed. As in the rest of Latin America, import-substitution industrialization proved to be a dead end. Fewer finished goods were imported, but large amounts of raw materials and intermediate products still needed to be imported for the industrialization process. The small market size and inefficiencies of production made Central American industrial products expensive and unable to compete with cheaper goods made elsewhere unless their producers were protected by high tariffs. Before long, the Central American businessmen found themselves in the familiar situation of producing inferior goods at uncompetitive prices. They lobbied governments to protect them in their domestic markets and were unable to export to help the countries earn valuable foreign exchange. This situation continued until the oil shock of 1973, when escalating oil prices created balance of payments crises in all the Central American countries.

This sequence of events proved to be an explosive combination. The import-substitution industrialization of the 1960s and early 1970s had produced the appearance of prosperity in urban areas, while aggravating the desperate conditions of the rural masses. The unequal distribution of income became even more glaring. Urban workers and national businessmen who had profited during the import substitution years suddenly found their economic fortunes reversed in the late 1970s and sought political solutions of the left and right to preserve their economic positions. Traditional elites responded in their customary fashion by pushing the lid down tighter on a political stew near the boiling point. Indifference and neglect by the United States, demands by peasants, workers, the Church, and elements of the middle class for a say in their future, and the stake of Cuba and the Soviet Union in disruption of the status quo created the fatal mix.

A Conflict Low-Intensity in Name Only

By the mid-1980s, the United States was fighting wars—by advice and proxies—in two Central American countries, and preparing a third—Honduras—as a base of supply should its own troops need to be used in the future. The name given to the politico-military strategy behind this U.S. involvement is "low-intensity conflict (LIC)." LIC is a doctrine that seeks to apply to Central America lessons learned from Vietnam. The lessons are that counterinsurgency wars in the Third World are "total" wars that require political, psychological, economic, and military components *and* that U.S. public opinion cannot sustain long-term, high-level, direct commitments of the country's armed forces. The support of local armies fighting guerrilla forces, as in El Salvador, and of rebel groups seeking to overthrow Marxist governments, as in Nicaragua, is central to this strategy.

The intensity of LIC is low, however, only in terms of U.S. casualties. Perhaps as many as 150,000 Central Americans have lost their lives in war-related violence since 1980. The equivalent in terms of the U.S. population would be over 1,000,000.

Yet the costs for the United States are anything but insignificant. For political leaders, Central America has become the most divisive issue since Vietnam, and has occupied more time of the president and Congress than any other foreign policy question. Official estimates of U.S. aid to the region were running by the late 1980s at nearly $1.5 billion annually and unofficial calculations set the figure at three times that if military support activities were included. Most tragically of all, this aid, both military and economic, served only to help the region survive the costs of war and to barely maintain living standards that had dropped to levels of ten and twenty years earlier.

The Lessons of Central American History

This one-chapter history of Central America from Columbus to Castro cannot do justice to the complex experience of that region of the world. But the brief review does illustrate basic themes that are crucial to any discussion of the contemporary Central American crisis.

1. *Political Instability.* Given Central America's origins, it is not surprising that democratic political systems modeled on the United States or Western Europe did not develop. Except for Costa Rica, none of the countries of the region seem to have that peculiar set of political, economic, and social conditions that has produced democratic governments. But even more striking is the inability of any political formula, even nondemocratic, to achieve the minimal

goals of stability, economic progress, and the integration of the majority of the population into national life. Assigning historical blame is always a risky business. But Central America's political elites seem to bear responsibility for their failure to develop a vision of society that would produce a better future. Jealously guarding their short-term privileges, they have produced a situation that cannot endure indefinitely and is bound now to be influenced by actors outside their control, such as the United States, or Cuba and the Soviet Union.

2. *The Fragile Economy.* The artificiality of any division between politics and economics is reinforced by a reading of the history of Central America. Ever since the origins of Central America as a colony designed to produce wealth for mother Spain, economics has placed limits on possible political arrangements. These tiny countries, linked so tightly to the fluctuations of the international market, are highly vulnerable. Policies adopted in Washington or at an OPEC meeting can mean the difference literally between life and death for the poorest sectors of Central America's population.

This tense economic environment makes constructive political arrangements that much more difficult. Any attempts to democratize politics require assaults on the privileged positions of the economic elites, specifically, the breaking up of large estates and the redistribution of scarce land. While widely seen as desirable politically and socially, this disruption of agricultural production often decreases absolute output because of less efficient methods, or the natural tendency of the peasant to consume more of his product in his own meager diet. Unless followed up with credit facilities for seeds and fertilizers and extension services to teach proper farming methods, land reform can leave the peasants worse off than before. All this costs money that the Central American countries do not have.

3. *The Role of the United States.* Any review of the history of Central America suggests that, for better or worse, the United States has been preoccupied with that part of the world. It is the relative neglect of the area during the 1970s, not the heavy involvement of the 1980s, that seems atypical. The United States has certainly contributed to Central America's problems. The invasions and direct occupations of Central American countries early in this

century produced stability, but at the cost of dictatorships whose legacies are now being played out in the region.

In a perfect world, the Central American countries could work out their destinies free from outside interference. Who knows what unique combinations of political life would evolve to face the region's dilemmas? But that perfect world does not exist and has never existed. From their beginnings as independent states, the Central American countries have meddled in each others' affairs and have been the object of rivalries by the big powers.

The stakes in Central America in the 1980s were higher than ever. For reasons beyond its control, the region became a test case for U.S. resolve in a global chess match with the Soviet Union. Uncertain of the role it must play in the Third World, the United States dealt with Central America while attempting to reconstruct a foreign policy consensus that was shattered by the Vietnam experience.

Central American history has some hard lessons for the United States. Traditionally linked to the status quo, the United States will be viewed with hostility by many Central Americans seeking to remake their future. The United States is the logical scapegoat for the forces of nationalism and social change. Radical movements will be likely to imitate the Sandinistas and view the Yankee as the "enemy of humanity."

Neglectful of the region for so long and content to let friendly dictators deal with Central America's glaring problems in their own style, the United States must now play catch-up. In El Salvador, it chose to back moderate reform, to tolerate the traditional right, and to attempt to exclude the radical left. Elsewhere in the region, the United States was less clear about which side it was on, encouraging civilian democracies, but barely addressing the underlying social and economic tensions. In the case of Nicaragua, the Reagan administration was convinced that the Sandinistas must go, but unable to devise a strategy to achieve that goal at acceptable political costs.

History tells us that the United States has often taken Central America for granted. In the shadow of the United States, Central America was an area of the world that could be relied on as being safe and secure for U.S. interests with little expenditure of money or manpower. That situation has now changed. The United States faces a difficult and fateful choice in Central America. It can seek to restore the isthmus to its former compliant position, with all the political and military costs that entails. Alternatively, it can try to create some new way of coexisting with its southern neighbors that places the United States on the side of social, political, and economic change. However, this alternative runs the risk that, in surrendering control of the region, the United States will be forced to deal with regimes that challenge important U.S. interests.

Notes

1. An *hacienda* was a special kind of agricultural institution that developed in much of Latin America. Largely self-sufficient, it differed from a plantation in that it did not specialize in the production of a cash crop for export to external markets. *Haciendas* and plantations in Latin America contributed to the development of two other phenomena, *minifundio* and *latifundio*. *Minifundio* (literally, tiny plots) is the division of the small amounts of land available to the peasants into plots too small to be efficient or to support the families dependent on them. *Latifundio* is the corresponding problem of large, underutilized estates maintained by the aristocracy. Strictly speaking, the hacienda reached its greatest development in the nineteenth century, but the social pressures created by the elite's monopolization of land existed in various forms from the earliest decades of the Spanish conquest.

2. Grin´go, n.; gringos [Sp., gibberish] Among Spanish-Americans, an Englishman or American; hostile and contemptuous term.

3. While Latin Americans in private and sometimes in public refer to citizens of the United States by the less than complimentary term *gringo*, they object when U.S. citizens refer to themselves as "Americans." They argue, quite rightly, that all inhabitants of the Western Hemisphere are Americans and that it is arrogant of those from North America to reserve the term to themselves. The moral is that if you don't want to be called a *gringo*, it helps to acknowledge that you're a *North* American.

4. Man´ifest Des´tiny. The nineteenth-century doctrine that it is the destiny of the Anglo-Saxon nations, especially of the United States, to dominate the entire Western Hemisphere.
5. Ralph Lee Woodward, Jr., *Central America, A Nation Divided* (New York: Oxford University Press, 1976), pp. 175–76.
6. Stephen Schlesinger and Stephen Kinzer, *Bitter Fruit* (Garden City, N.Y.: Anchor Books, 1983), p. 68.

2

Central American "Snapshots"

Nicaragua: A Revolution Besieged

El Tigre, Nicaragua—Rifle fire crackled in nearby trees and echoed ominously across the sunbaked valley, but none of the rebel fighters reached for his weapon.

The shots came from other rebels hunting deer for dinner, the contras explained as they dozed in the high-noon heat by a shack in this hamlet. There was no risk of attack by Sandinista government troops, the drowsy contras said.

Deer-hunting was a luxury the contras rarely enjoyed before the 60-day ceasefire agreement signed March 23 in Sapoa. The pact formalized a truce, now five weeks old, that was widely respected across the country by both sides, bringing Nicaraguans an extraordinary respite from six years of fighting.

Across the battle-worn Pantasma Valley in northern Jinotega province, civilian villagers and contra and Sandinista troops spoke of nascent possibilities for economic improvement and political reconciliation that the truce has encouraged. But they also said the conflict's rancor and suffering are far from forgotten, and many predicted that the killing would begin again.

"This is sixty days of happiness," said Anna María Escoto, a withered peasant mother who was visiting her Sandinista soldier son at an Army camp at Asturias, south of Pantasma.

"If we're not dancing, it's because we're exhausted from war," she said. "If we're not whistling, it's because our throats are dry from so much pain."

—Julia Preston, *Washington Post*, April 26, 1988

Following the triumph of a popular revolution in July 1979, most Nicaraguans shared great hopes for a new Nicaragua, without the despised Somoza. Although some 90 percent of the population was united in its opposition to Somoza, Nicaraguans were not in agreement on a future economic and political system to replace that

47

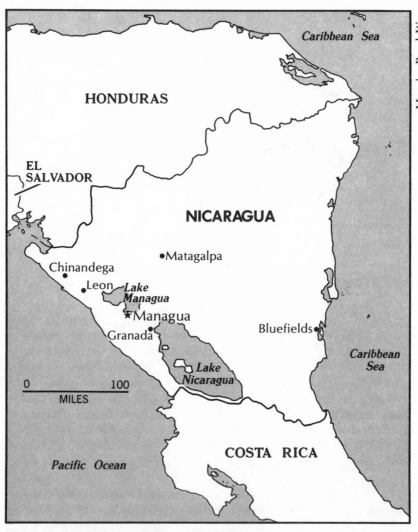

dominated by the Somoza dynasty. Leaving aside the die-hard reactionaries who never stopped fighting the Sandinistas, there were three competing visions of post-Somoza Nicaragua. The Sandinista leaders, a mix of nationalists and Marxist-Leninists, were determined to restructure Nicaraguan economic and political life to serve the interests of the poor majority. They believed that socialism was the system most appropriate to achieving this goal. But, given Nicaragua's backward state, a private sector, carefully controlled, would be needed in a "mixed" economy—part private, part socialized. Internationally, Nicaragua would be "anti-imperialist" (read, anti–United States) and "nonaligned," but with strong ties to socialist countries. A second group, while sympathetic to the Sandinistas' goal of helping the poor, placed priority on political change and wanted to establish something that had never existed before in Nicaragua: a democratic system like that in neighboring Costa Rica, with a strong private sector and a friendly attitude toward the United States. A third group, part of the traditional ruling class, was less concerned about economic justice or political freedom and wanted to overthrow Somoza to gain a larger piece of the political and economic pie for themselves. This group looked to a close alliance with the United States.

The Sandinista National Liberation Front (FSLN) began armed opposition to Somoza in 1961. For more than a decade the FSLN had only limited success in hit-and-run attacks. A natural disaster turned events in its favor. After an earthquake devastated Managua in 1972, leaving 10,000 dead, Somoza channeled international humanitarian aid into his own pockets. The upper and professional classes, who had shared in Somoza's economic development of the 1950s and 1960s, felt that corruption and political favoritism had finally reached intolerable levels and began to turn against Somoza. The catalytic event was the January 1978 murder by Somoza's henchmen of one of Nicaragua's most prominent citizens, Pedro Joaquín Chamorro Cardenal, editor of the opposition newspaper, *La Prensa*. Chamorro had led many failed rebellions against Somoza and represented the most respected and viable alternative to the Sandinistas. Some 30,000 Nicaraguans turned out for Chamorro's funeral, and professionals, businessmen, and unions began a series of strikes demanding Somoza's fall. Despite overwhelming opposition, the dictator held on to the last, issuing orders from his bunker to the hated National Guard to bomb cities sympathetic to the Sandinistas. But bombing alone could not stop a nation seemingly united to overthrow him. With the Sandinistas at the gates of Managua, Somoza took U.S. advice and fled. The revolution left 40,000 to 50,000 dead, 100,000 wounded, 40,000 orphans, and an estimated $1.3 billion in war damages. Enormous foreign loans had been contracted and the treasury looted to support Somoza's golden exile in Miami.

The first postrevolutionary government was a five-member junta that included two non-Sandinistas. But the Sandinistas called the shots, as those with the guns in a revolution inevitably do, through a directorate composed of the nine Sandinista *comandantes*, and presented their decisions to the junta. Relations between the increasingly arrogant and doctrinaire Sandinistas and the democratic and nondemocratic opposition quickly went from lukewarm to sour in the summer of 1980. The legislative body, the Council of State, was reduced to a consultative body in May and was stacked with appointed members from the abundant Sandinista mass organizations. Most non-Sandinistas resigned in protest. Censorship of any news remotely connected to the economy or the contra war began in August 1980. The two non-Sandinista members of the junta resigned in April 1980, and were replaced with two other non-Sandinistas, including future opposition leader Arturo Cruz. In August 1980, the Sandinistas announced that, contrary to expectations outside Nicaragua, elections would not be held until 1985, and campaigning would not be allowed until 1984.

As Nicaraguans divided among themselves over the future direction of Nicaragua, U.S.-Sandinista relations, never easy, grew increasingly contentious. The legacy of U.S. involvement in Nicaragua gave the Sandinistas ample reason not to trust the "Colossus of the North." The United States had invaded and occupied Nicaragua in the 1920s and 1930s and had handpicked Somoza to head the despised National Guard. From the point of view of the Sandinistas, the United States had stood by its loyal but brutal ally as he ordered the National Guard to defeat the Sandinistas at any cost. Internally divided, the Carter administration wavered, but did not try to remove Somoza until the Sandinistas were practically at the doors of the dictator's bunker. When the United States finally decided that Somoza was a liability, it tried, unsuccessfully, to mediate the removal of Somoza in order to prevent the Sandinistas from coming to power. When no other Latin American state would join its mediation efforts in the Organization of American States (OAS), the United States settled for a series of vague promises from the Sandinistas about respect for human rights, democracy, and a mixed economy.

Once the Sandinistas assumed power, the Carter administration made conciliatory overtures, designed to moderate the revolution, by sending $8 million in disaster relief, supporting Nicaragua's loan requests from multilateral financial institutions, and requesting $75 million in economic assistance from Congress. The Sandinistas were not impressed with the administration's efforts. Congress held up the economic request for seven months, and the bulk of the initial aid went to nongovernmental, private enterprises and Catholic Church organizations.

For its part, the United States was impatient with the Sandinistas' postponement of elections, the growing Cuban and Eastern-bloc presence, and the militarization of Nicaragua. In the last days of his administration, Carter charged the Sandinistas with arming the Salvadoran guerrillas, suspended the aid package, and blocked international financial loans. Despite evidence that aid to the Salvadoran guerrillas had decreased in response to this suspension under the Carter administration, the new Reagan administration canceled the assistance in April 1981. In November 1981, the United States Congress authorized the CIA to assist covertly counterrevolutionary groups already operating against the Sandinistas. The congressional authorization was ostensibly to assist the "contras" (called *contrarevolucionarios* or counterrevolutionaries) to deter Sandinista support for the guerrillas in El Salvador. The contras themselves stated from the beginning that their goal was to overthrow the Sandinistas.

In June 1983, after authorizing some $80 million in aid to the contras over the previous two years, Congress cut funding for the covert activity. Nevertheless, the contras, some 500 strong in 1981, had grown to 15,000 by the late 1980s and had broadened their political and military base. Not able to occupy any Nicaraguan territory, the contras operated out of bases in Honduras and Costa Rica. They caused great loss of life (and were charged with the deaths of innocent civilians), disrupted important economic activities such as the coffee harvest, and required the Sandinistas to institute an unpopular draft and to increase the porportion of the government budget going to military spending to some 50 percent.

Despite the existence of both political and armed opposition, the Sandinistas continued to have many supporters. The country's poor majority benefited from a government designed to serve their interests and are the prime supporters of the revolution. The Sandinistas initiated a successful literacy campaign and dramatically improved rural health care during the early years of the revolution. Those under the age of sixteen—nearly half the population—are among the most ardent supporters of the Sandinistas, though the military draft has created protest and "draft dodgers" among some.

Presidental and legislative elections were held earlier than expected, in 1984, with limited participation by opposition groups. After several months of haggling with the Sandinistas over campaign conditions, a key opposition coalition, the Democratic Coordinator, chose not to field its presidential candidate, Arturo Cruz. They complained that government censorship of the press and radio and the long-standing prohibition on campaigning and holding public rallies for nongovernment groups, although reduced or suspended in the period immediately preceding the vote, did not permit fair elections. The Sandinista candidate for president, Daniel Ortega, won 68 percent of the vote. Some parties critical of the Sandinistas from the right and the left did participate and received some 30 percent of the ballots and representation in the legislature. Some *comandantes* described the elections as a "bourgeois formality" for foreign consumption, which could not determine who held power, and argued that the Sandinista victory in the revolution gave the FSLN all the legitimacy it needed. But the government did proceed to draft a new constitution with the collaboration of the seven political parties in the new national assembly.

In 1985, U.S.-Nicaraguan relations became both more tense and more confused. Despite massive lobbying by the administration, Congress at first rejected continued aid to the contras, though some members successfully encouraged the president to use his emergency powers to declare an economic embargo against Nicaragua. When the Sandinistas gave continued signs of pursuing closer relations with one of their remaining allies, the Soviet Union, many in Congress who had opposed direct military aid to the contras voted for $27 million in aid for "humanitarian" purposes. The U.S. aid for food, clothing, and medical supplies kept the rebels in business by allowing them to channel funds raised privately to the purchase of weapons without direct U.S. involvement. Internally, the Sandinistas prepared to move forcefully against the contras by evacuating tens of thousands from border areas to create Sandinista "free fire zones." Border incidents with Honduras and Costa Rica increased, and the contra war escalated in ferocity. Speculation that the United States was seeking a pretext for direct military involvement, officially denied in Washington, abounded in Nicaragua. A drive to defeat the contras within a year served the Sandinistas as justification of the suspension of remaining civil liberties in October of 1985.

The cycle of war and violence and of deteriorating U.S.-Nicaraguan relations spun out of control in 1986. Through a massive lobbying effort the Reagan administration reversed the slim margin of opposition to contra aid in the House of Representatives and in June achieved the highest level of lethal aid to that point: $100 million. The day after approval of the aid, the Sandinista government ordered the indefinite closing of La Prensa, a symbol for many of political freedom inside Nicaragua.

The death and destruction visited upon Nicaragua by the contra war mounted. Crippled by the U.S. trade embargo and unable to fully replace declining production and exports with either Western or Eastern-bloc aid, Nicaragua printed money to pay for the costs of a war that was reported to have inflicted $3 billion in damages on the economy. The result was runaway inflation (over 2,000 percent by 1988), shortages of food and essential goods, and rampant speculation, corruption, and black market activity. By 1988 perhaps as many as 50,000 Nicaraguans (contra, Sandinista, and civilian) had been killed in the guerrilla war.

Change in Washington in late 1986 began the reversal of the downward slide for Nicaragua. From the perspective of the 1990s two events will probably be seen as key: the return of the Senate to Democratic control in November of 1986 and the revelations that same month of arms sales to Iran and the diversion of profits to evade Congressional restrictions on funding for the contras. The investigations of the so-called "Iran-Contra Affair" (see box, "Iran, Contra: An Affair to Remember," pp. 54–59), had minimal effects on the domestic political scene and even served as a platform for Col. Oliver North, dismissed National Security Council aide, to make impassioned pleas for contra aid. But the combination of

IRAN-CONTRA: AN AFFAIR TO REMEMBER

On November 3, 1986 the Lebanese magazine, *Al Shiraa*, startled the U.S. government and most of the North American public. A lead article stated that the Reagan Administration, which had maintained a hard line on terrorism by opposing any negotiations with terrorists and by bombing Libya to demonstrate its resolve, had sold weapons to Iran. Ordinary citizens and seasoned analysts were shocked again when, after initial denials, President Reagan admitted that there had, indeed, been an arms deal between his Administration and the Khomeini government in hopes of strengthening ties with moderates within that regime. He stressed, however, that, "We did not, repeat did not, trade weapons or anything else for hostages, nor will we."

Later that month a team appointed by Attorney General Edwin Meese to investigate the affair announced an unexpected twist. A memorandum found in National Security Council files documented that profits made from U.S. arms sales to Iran in 1985 and 1986 were used to fund the contra army fighting the Sandinista government of Nicaragua. While the news surprised many citizens, it outraged members of the U.S. Congress, which had voted to curtail all aid to the contras during this period and had enacted legislation that many believed legally prohibited the U.S. government from lending support to the rebels. Further investigations uncovered an intricate secret network headquartered at the National Security Council that solicited and delivered funds and supplies to the contras from private individuals and allied governments. This covert network, employing U.S. government officials and their agents, spanned several continents and quietly functioned without the knowledge or consent of congressional committees normally privy to such information.

The political and constitutional crisis known as the Iran-contra affair had begun. The public, the media, Congress, and the various commissions appointed to investigate the affair brimmed with questions: Had the president approved of an arms-for-hostage swap with the Iranians? What did the president know about this top-secret network that sold weapons to a "terrorist state" and siphoned profits to rebel allies in Central America? If he did know about these activities, when did he know? If he was not aware of these activities, who was, and why did they keep the president in the dark? Had the administration violated the Constitution by circumventing Congress to aid the contra rebels during this period? Did the Boland Amendment, the law enacted by Congress to restrict U.S. government involvement in contra activities, apply to the National Security Council or was that body beyond the purview of the legislation?

A number of official bodies were named to find answers to these and other questions. Shortly after Meese assembled his investigative team at the Justice Department, the FBI was called in to assist. On December 19, in order to avoid a possible conflict of interest, investigation of possible criminal activity related to the affair was transferred from the Justice Department to Independent Counsel Lawrence Walsh. The President also appointed a three-member board chaired by former Senator John Tower (R-Tex.) to make an independent study and to publish its findings. Early in 1987 the House of Representatives formed the Select Committee to Investigate Covert Arms Transactions with Iran, and the Senate named members to its Select Committee on Secret Military Assistance to Iran and the Nicaraguan Opposition, in order to reach their own conclusions about the events. On May 5, twenty-six legislators from both houses of Congress joined together to conduct hearings on the matter.

Attorney General Meese's initial "fact-finding" inquiry came under harsh attack for overlooking many important investigative tasks that would have negative effects on ensuing research into the matter. The team included no criminal investigators, and Meese neglected to ask key senior officials many pertinent questions, nor did he take notes of his meetings with these officials. The error that had perhaps the greatest effect on the overall Iran-contra investigation was his failure to secure key White House documentation regarding the covert activities. Because of this error, then–National Security Adviser Rear Admiral John Poindexter was able to destroy pertinent documents, and NSC staffer Lieutenant Colonel Oliver North, along with his secretary Fawn Hall, secretly carried out the now-famous "shredding party" in North's National Security Council office at the Executive Office Building. A number of documents that would have helped establish a more accurate understanding of the chain of command and sequence of events in the Iran-contra affair were thus altered or destroyed.

However, defenders of the attorney general argue that it was Meese who originally established that a diversion of funds had occurred and that the President had been unaware of this—two central conclusions of both the Congressional and Tower Commission investigations.

The Tower Commission issued its report on February 26, 1987, clearing the President of any wrongdoing and blaming instead high Administration officials for carrying out sensitive activities without the knowledge of the President. The Commission did criticize the President's "hands-off" management style for allowing serious breaches of professional conduct to occur during his tenure.

The most extensive airing of the Iran-contra affair was carried out by Congress. For nearly three months during the summer of 1987 citizens watched or read about the often riveting and contradictory testimony given by the twenty-nine witnesses about the arms-for-hostages deal, the ensuing diversion of "residuals" to the contras, and the byzantine workings of the covert network that carried it out.

The kingpins in the affair turned out to be, among others, former National Security Advisers Robert McFarlane and Rear Admiral John Poindexter, CIA Director William Casey (who died of a brain tumor before he was able to testify), and National Security Council staffer Marine Lieutenant-Colonel Oliver North. Retired Air Force Major-General Richard Secord and Iranian-American businessman Albert Hakim, who served as middlemen in the arms transfer, also testified as key witnesses at the hearings. North and Poindexter, among others, received limited immunity from prosecution in exchange for their testimony.

The president did not testify before the Iran-contra committee hearings, but he publicly maintained that the first shipment of TOW antitank missiles to Iran in November 1985 was not intended to be an exchange for hostages. However, a presidential "finding"—the written executive authorization required for covert operations—signed in December 1985 by the President (designed to be retroactive to cover past as well as future weapons sales) clearly stated that the weapons transfer was meant to gain freedom for U.S. hostages.

The December finding was one of the documents Poindexter destroyed before Meese's investigators secured it. The former presidential adviser maintains that he destroyed the evidence in order to save the president from implication in the affair. President Reagan eventually concluded that he could not recall signing such a document. In an ironic paraphrasing of Harry S. Truman's famous statement that responsibility rests with the president, Poindexter took responsibility by declaring, "On this whole issue, you know, the buck stops here with me."

President Reagan's final judgment on the affair, made in May, 1987, was that "no laws had been broken," but that what had transpired had not been his original intent. "A few months ago, I told the American people I did not trade arms for hostages. My heart and my best intentions still tell me that's true, but the facts and evidence tell me it is not."

Constitutional disputes between the executive and legislative branches flared over whether the so-called Boland Amendment had been violated. This legislation, which was enacted in various versions between 1984 and 1986, prohibited any government agency involved in intelligence activities from providing the contras with military aid. White House counsel and prominent conservative legal scholars, as well as Oliver North and other Iran-contra principals, maintain that the National Security Council, which directed the contra support operations, should not be considered an intelligence agency and was therefore not covered by the Boland Amendment. The Iran-contra committee stated in its final report that both the letter and spirit of this law had been violated. Speaker of the House Jim Wright (D-Tex.) charged that the law had been "flouted." Former National Security Adviser Robert McFarlane (who preceded John Poindexter in the post) testified that he understood the law to apply to the National Security Council, and claimed at the Iran-contra hearings that because of this legal restriction he had ordered his staff not to raise funds for the contras. North asserted that he had never heard any such order.

Oliver North, John Poindexter, Under Secretary of State for Inter-American Affairs Elliott Abrams, and other Iran-contra witnesses, admitted that they had lied to and/or misled Congress about administration involvement with the contras during the 1984–86 hiatus of Congressional funding of the rebels. Because they feared that members of Congress would move to block activities they considered vital to the nation's security, they had felt justified in failing to inform Congress in a timely manner as required by law. Oliver North claimed in testimony that he and other high-level officials did not believe that Congress could be trusted to maintain the secrecy of sensitive covert operations.

Those involved in the Iran-contra affair said that they had assumed that their actions met with or would have met with the President's approval—if he had known of them. No witness testified that Reagan had ordered or even knew of the diversion of funds to the contras or of any other breach of the law. For high-level officials such as Poindexter and Casey, who had allegedly kept the affair from the president, Reagan's well-known devotion to the contra cause was proof enough of his potential support for their project. By keeping him in the dark they were shielding him from political harm should the covert operations become public. Lower-level participants such as Oliver North claimed that Poindexter and Casey had led them to believe the president was fully informed of the diversion of funds and other contra support activity, and that he had given his specific approval.

Two-hundred-fifty hours of testimony, 250,000 pages of documents, and 1,059 official exhibits later, Senator Daniel Inouye (D-Hawaii) closed the joint hearings stating that the Iran-contra story "has now been told." He went on to say that this "chilling" tale of "deceit, duplicity and arrogant disregard of the rule of law" was incomplete and that the U.S. public may never fully learn what had transpired nor why.

Despite the contradictions between the testimony of many of the witnesses and political disagreements among the bipartisan committee members (seventeen of the twenty-nine committee members were contra aid supporters), all seemed to agree that the President had been involved in the sale of weapons to Iran for the purpose of freeing U.S. hostages, but that he had not been aware of the transfer of "residual" funds to the contras. They embraced the story that "fall guy" Oliver North, John Poindexter, and William Casey were responsible for the worst of the illegal acts. The final report states: "These committees found no evidence suggesting that the President was a knowing participant in the effort to deceive Congress and the American public. But the President's actions and statements contributed to the deception."

More than six months after the close of the congressional inquiry, Special Prosecutor Lawrence Walsh, on the basis of information independently collected during a fourteen-month grand jury investigation, brought indictments against North, Poindexter, Secord, and Hakim for their roles in the affair. In the most sweeping criminal action levied against White House officials since the Watergate scandal, the twenty-three-count indictment charged the men with, among other criminal acts, "conspiracy to defraud the United States government by illegally providing the Nicaraguan rebels with profits from the sale of weapons to Iran."

The men and women who participated in the Iran-contra affair believed that their actions were of vital importance to the security of the United States, and that the contras represented the country's best defense against the spread of communism in Central America. Some who have come to their defense have argued that the Iran-contra debacle was not at all like the other national political scandal to which it is often compared: Watergate. In the Watergate break-in and cover-up, laws were violated to advance the personal and political ambitions of President Nixon and his advisers. As Fawn Hall suggested in her testimony before Congress, a "higher law" operated in Iran-contra: defense of the security interests of the United States.

Critics of those who participated in the Iran-contra activities point out that one's particular political beliefs and convictions must not override the rule of law and system of checks and balances that serve as the basis of the American government and way of life. Secretary of State George Shultz, who remained unscathed by the scandal, underscored this principle in his testimony before the Iran-contra committee. Regarding the sale of arms to Iran and the diversion of profits to the contras he said: "You cannot spend funds that Congress doesn't either authorize you to obtain or appropriate. That is what the Constitution says and we have to stick to it. . . ."

Perhaps in an attempt to prevent North Americans from suffering from the cynicism and lack of faith in their government that followed the Vietnam War and the Watergate scandal, Shultz commented:

> I want to send a message out around our country that public service is a very rewarding and honorable thing, and nobody has to think they need to lie and cheat in order to be a public servant or to work in foreign policy. Quite to the contrary, if you are really going to be effective over any period of time, you have to be straightforward and you have to conduct yourself in a basically honest way so people will have confidence and trust in you.

—Marta Iris Tanenhaus

domestic scandal and shifting political fortunes for the Republicans persuaded several Central American leaders and, eventually, the contras themselves to hedge their bets on future North American policy. Costa Rican President Oscar Arias launched a new peace initiative in early 1987 that led to a surprise agreement among the five Central American Presidents in August 1987. (See box, "The Central American Peace Proposals: A Perspective from the Year 2020," pp. 80–83.)

The new peace plan had its greatest impact in Nicaragua. With the active and highly controversial encouragement of Democratic House Speaker Jim Wright, President Daniel Ortega began a campaign to undercut contra support in the U.S. Congress and end the war. Democratic majorities in Congress defeated military aid to the contras in February 1988; in a political decision it would later regret, the Administration opposed a compromise nonlethal-aid package in March. Concessions by Nicaragua on domestic political freedoms and on direct talks with the contras caught the Reagan administration repeatedly off guard and shifted the struggle from the battlefield to a negotiating table inside Nicaragua in March 1988. Despite progress in the talks, the contras maintained that negotiations over a ceasefire and their reintegration into Nicaraguan political life were contingent on the installation of Western-style democracy in Nicaragua, and that they would wage war again if necessary.

Nicaragua is rich in arable land—although only 8 percent of the available land is being used—and is relatively underpopulated. Nine-tenths of the population live on the western slope of the country (where Spanish and *mestizo* heritages dominate); the rest of the population (English-speaking descendants of Jamaican slaves brought to cultivate bananas in the 1800s and descendants of the indigenous Misquito Indians) live on the Atlantic coast. Agriculture makes up 24 percent of the gross domestic product and accounts for 48 percent of the economically active population. Nicaragua exports cotton, coffee, sugar, beef, seafood, and bananas. Its beef is second only to Argentina's as the region's best. The economy remains mixed, with 30 percent of production in private hands, 30 percent belonging to peasant cooperatives with individual ownership of plots, and 40 percent in state hands. (Much of the state property consists of the Somoza dynasty's vast enterprises and land—some 20 percent of the land under cultivation—which was expropriated by the Sandinistas and turned into state or cooperative ventures.) Following the revolution, foreign economic assistance and development specialists from Western Europe and the Eastern bloc flowed into Nicaragua to try to offset economic problems caused by the war against Somoza. Except for U.S. aid to El Salvador, Nicaragua receives more assistance from countries in the West than any other Central American country.

KEY FACTS ABOUT NICARAGUA:*

Population: 3,500,000; 56 percent urban

Area: 50,193 square miles, or about the size of Iowa

Infant Mortality (1985): 69 deaths per 1,000 live births during the course of the first year of life

Per Capita Income (GNP, 1985): US $770

Size of Armed Forces (includes total armed forces, does not include reserves or paramilitary): 77,000

*Sources: see below, p. 90.

Literacy: 88 percent

President and next scheduled election: Commander Daniel Ortega
Saavedra took office in January 1985. The next scheduled
presidential election is in February 1990.

Total External Debt (in millions of dollars): US $5,615

Per Capita Military Spending: US $90

El Salvador: The End of the Middle Option?

El Salvador's international airport is the largest and most modern
in all of Central America. Located some fifty kilometers from the
capital, it sits surrounded by the green patchwork of divided and
subdivided plots of land that seem to occupy every square inch of
the country's overpopulated territory. Constructed in the 1970s, the
airport was placed so far from the capital to accommodate tourists,
for whom high-rise hotels had been constructed on the nearby
Pacific beaches. But instead of a tourist boom, the late 1970s
brought social disintegration and civil war to El Salvador. The high-
rise hotels are now mostly deserted and some, in guerrilla-con-
trolled territory, are completely shut down. The modern airport,
connected to San Salvador by the country's only four-lane super-
highway, serves as a convenience for the North Americans who
come to help fight or report on the war, not to visit the beaches.

El Salvador is the smallest and most densely populated country
in the region. There are 157.3 persons to the square mile, a greater
population density than in India. Overpopulation, coupled with a
lack of land and resources, contributed to a war with Honduras in
1969, the migration of several hundred thousand peasants to the
capital or to other countries, and the political-economic disaster of
the late 1970s and early 1980s. The population has been traditionally concentrated in central and western El Salvador, where the
rich volcanic earth produces two of the country's principal exports,
coffee and cotton. The relatively underpopulated eastern provinces,
hotly disputed by the government and the guerrillas, are now
inhabited by only 10 percent of the population.

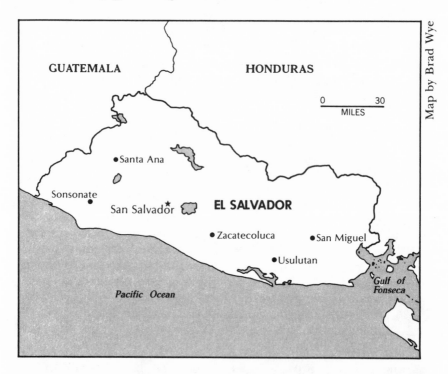

Before the war El Salvador was the most integrated and industrialized country in Central America, boasting light industry and an extensive structure of paved highways and railroads. Now, any trip begins with inquiries about which roads have been blown up by, or are under the control of, the guerrillas.

Along the roadside are the *campesinos* (peasants) who live miserable lives even in the best of times. Until recently, 2 percent of the population owned 60 percent of the land. Although nationalization of 22 percent of the land under a 1980 reform law has somewhat reduced the concentration of land in the hands of the few, severe land shortages and sharecropping conditions prevail. Many *campesinos* are migrant workers, who follow the harvests in order to earn subsistence wages. For the *campesinos* who live on new cooperatives created by the agrarian reform program, life is better. ·But lack of credits and of technical assistance still threatens the viability of areas affected by the reform. Phase II of the land reform program, designed to distribute the most productive, coffee-producing land, has never been implemented.

Human development did not accompany El Salvador's considerable industrialization in the 1960s and 1970s: per-capita income is among the lowest in the region. The majority of the country does not have access to safe drinking water. Mothers have no choice but to give their babies foul water that may well cause diarrhea and dehydration and add another statistic to El Salvador's infant mortality rate. Access to health care is available through church relief workers and doctors who risk their lives by caring for the poor. Those who help the poor are considered to be "subversive" by the army and the right, and have been frequent targets of the death squads.

Access to primary education, always minimal outside the cities, has deteriorated since the war began; teachers don't want to go where bullets fly. Half the population is illiterate. Nevertheless, there are more radio stations and a higher newspaper readership in El Salvador than in any other Central American country.

In El Salvador, it is almost impossible to find anyone, regardless of his or her background, who has not lost a loved one to one side or the other since 1979. Even the wealthy are not immune to killings and kidnappings by the guerrillas. But the poor have been hit the hardest by the war. Poor people are trapped in the middle, and most families have suffered abuses from both sides, often repeatedly. Both the guerrillas and the army suspect those who hesitate to demonstrate their loyalty. Although political deaths have greatly decreased (5,331 in 1982; 1,677 in 1983; some 800 in 1984; 335 in 1985; 248 in 1986; according to State Department figures) and limited democracy has come, it is still dangerous to express a preference for the left. Particularly desperate are the more than 500,000 displaced Salvadorans who live in makeshift camps and are continually suspect as guerrilla sympathizers.

The guerrillas number 5,000 to 7,000 and are supported logistically by *las masas* (the masses). The *masas* are civilians (largely peasants) who provide the guerrillas with food, clothing, and shelter, serve as messengers and sources of information, and give other support necessary to their operations. U.S. government counterinsurgency experts estimate that for every guerrilla there are approximately ten *masas*, or roughly 1 percent of the population, who are active supporters of the guerrillas.

The Salvadoran guerrillas are composed of a military side, the

Farabundo Martí Liberation Front (FMLN), and a political side, the Democratic Revolutionary Front (FDR). The FMLN, consisting of five guerrilla groups, takes its name from 1930s Communist peasant leader Farabundo Martí, who died in the bloody *matanza* (massacre) of 1932. The FDR-FMLN represents a variety of political ideologies, from center-left democrats to a majority of Marxist-Leninists, with different views about the best road to power.

The conditions to produce a social upheaval in El Salvador had existed for decades: poverty among the masses, extreme wealth for a tiny oligarchy, brutal repression, and corrupt politics. The spark to light the fuse of revolution proved to be the rapid economic growth that came to El Salvador in the 1960s and 1970s. The country's tiny middle class was strengthened and expanded by the economic activity, but found it had no political representation. The traditional oligarchy tried to maintain its hold on political power by enlisting the military to protect its interests. Nineteen seventy-two proved to be a fateful year. José Napoleón Duarte, the reformist Christian Democratic mayor of San Salvador, stood for president with a running mate, Guillermo Ungo, who represented a block of left, socialist, and communist parties. Duarte and Ungo won the election but lost the count when the military suspended the election returns running in Duarte's favor and announced their own candidate as the winner. After leading an abortive coup against the military's theft of the election, Duarte was imprisoned, tortured, and exiled. The United States, which would later regret a missed opportunity, did nothing to support this peaceful attempt at reform by Duarte and Ungo.

Given the failure of the ballot to achieve change, "popular organizations" of peasants, workers, students, church sectors, and some elements of the middle class adopted nontraditional means of protest. Their land seizures, strikes, and peaceful factory and foreign embassy sit-ins were met with violent repression.

The Salvadoran civil war began in earnest after the October 1979 coup led by reformist military officers against the military dictator, Carlos Humberto Romero. Younger officers had been shocked by the overthrow of Somoza in nearby Nicaragua and feared that, unless basic reforms were instituted, social pressures in El Salvador could lead to a similar explosion and the demise of the armed forces. They followed an old dictum of the Latin American military that when the bulls are stampeding it is safer to lead them onto higher ground than to try to turn them from their course. Better, they thought, to lead a reform than to try to hold back a revolution. Inviting civilians into the junta, the military announced an extensive land-reform program and the nationalization of the country's banks and the coffee export trade.

Their reformist coup, however, unleashed the pent-up forces of El Salvador's highly polarized society. Some on the left used the political opening to try to push for more drastic changes and others for a true socialist revolution. The traditional right and more conservative officers sought to reverse the reformist moves of the younger officers and initiated a massive repression employing the infamous *escuadrones de muerte* (death squads)—paramilitary gangs linked to the military and orchestrated by the oligarchy—that turned El Salvador into a slaughterhouse. Each morning in San Salvador found new piles of brutally murdered and mutilated bodies on street corners, garbage dumps, and at the bottom of ravines.

Among the dead were many of the leaders of El Salvador's "popular organizations." This program of political assassination radicalized some leaders who had often been considered moderate in the Salvadoran context. Guillermo Ungo, Duarte's former running mate in 1972, left the reformist junta, eventually to become the chief spokesperson for the guerrillas' political arm, the FDR. Rubén Zamora, at one time a member of Duarte's party and a cabinet member of the reformist junta, abandoned democratic politics when his brother, Mario, the country's attorney general, was assassinated in his home while Rubén slept next door. He would join Ungo in representing the FDR/FMLN internationally.

Although many of the reformist junta's early supporters went into opposition when they felt the junta had been fatally compromised by repression and the resurgence of right wing officers, Duarte and the United States did not. Fearing a complete victory by the left, the United States rushed assistance to the Salvadoran military and attempted to shore up a government on the point of collapse. Total U.S. aid to El Salvador had been $16.8 million from 1946 to 1979. In 1980 and early 1981 the Carter administration delivered $10.7 million in "nonlethal" and lethal military aid plus a substantial economic-assistance package.

The salvage operation worked after a fashion. A "general offensive" by the guerrillas, modeled after the Sandinista victory in Nicaragua and designed to present President Reagan with a fait accompli on his inauguration, failed to spark the mass uprising that the guerrillas had expected. Additional military "trainers" from the United States and $25 million in military aid demonstrated in March 1981 that President Reagan was also committed to backing the civilian-military junta. Duarte, not much more than a figurehead for the military, had his reformist credentials severely tested as he presided over one of the most repressive periods in El Salvador's bloody history in 1980 and 1981.

Constituent Assembly elections in March 1982 produced a victory for a coalition of right-wing parties led by former major Roberto D'Aubuisson's ARENA party. Only strong pressure from the United States prevented D'Aubuisson from being named as provisional president. D'Aubuisson, who had been cashiered from the army because of his extreme politics, represented a far-right-wing response to El Salvador's civil war. Rumored to be linked directly to the death squads and to the murder of Archbishop Oscar Romero, a liberal church leader, D'Aubuisson was viewed as an unacceptable partner for the United States by much of the U.S. Congress. His party enjoyed popular support, however, in the countryside among landowners and some of the peasantry, and with the urban business sector. Though tarnished by his extremist reputation, ARENA would remain a strong brake on attempts at continuing the reforms of the 1979 junta.

With support from the United States and reported CIA funding, Duarte was elected president of El Salvador for the second time in 1984 and, this time, allowed to take office. Hamstrung by a Legislative Assembly dominated by the right wing, Duarte struggled throughout 1984 to gain the confidence of the armed forces, put the guerrillas on the defensive, and restore his image as a reformist politician. Amid grave economic reversals and predictions of defeat for his Christian Democratic party, Duarte emerged the surprising victor from new legislative and municipal elections in 1985, perhaps because of his equally unexpected, and so far unproductive, opening to the guerrillas in late 1984. D'Aubuisson and the traditional right received a crushing defeat at the polls and entered into a period of reexamination that led to D'Aubuisson's removal as leader of ARENA. Attacked by the wounded right as having stolen the election for the Christian Democrats, the military found itself in the pleasant but historically unprecedented position of defender of the democratic process. Whether the military has forsaken its bloody past for the way of democracy or merely made a marriage of convenience with the political arrangement most likely to guarantee its continued influence is a key question for the country's future.

In 1985, El Salvador was more stable politically than it had been for years. Its popular president seemed to be fulfilling his vision of himself as the savior of his country. The U.S. Congress continued to be pleased by the progress made politically and militarily and willing to maintain funding that had become crucial to El Salvador's daily survival. From 1981 to 1988, U.S. military and economic assistance to El Salvador totaled over $3 billion, making this tiny country of five million people the fifth largest recipient of U.S. aid in the world.

By mid-1985 there were signs that a politically and militarily weaker guerrilla movement was changing strategy. Political assassinations and kidnappings, targeted on North Americans as well as Salvadorans, increased, and the mobilization of workers and other "popular forces" that had been so prominent in 1979–80 reappeared. The air war against the guerrillas became a key element of the counterinsurgency strategy, while opponents of the policy raised concerns about possible civilian casualties and forced evacuations.

In retrospect 1985 may well be seen as the high point of administration policy in El Salvador. The decline of Duarte's fortunes began in earnest with a severe economic austerity program urged on him by the United States in early 1986. Urban labor, one of Duarte's strongest supporters, responded to the attack on real wages with some of the first mass demonstrations since the early 1980s. Natural disaster followed man-made ones: in October two devastating earthquakes struck the capital city, leaving 1,500 dead, 150,000 homeless, and $1 billion in damage.

Military optimism that the guerrillas were on the defensive was shattered by a series of isolated but effective attacks. One in March

1987 on a brigade headquarters in El Paraíso took the lives of at least 64 Salvadoran soldiers and the first American trainer to die in combat.

The Central American Peace Plan of August 7 altered the political equation in El Salvador as it had in other parts of Central America, but only temporarily. Talks between the government and the guerrillas, suspended since 1984, were renewed. Rubén Zamora and Guillermo Ungo, exiled leaders of the FDR, returned briefly in November to test the guarantees of political expression mandated by the Peace Plan. But more sinister developments occurred as well. With the resurgence of protest activities by students and labor groups, human rights violations began to escalate again. Confrontational tactics by supporters of the left did not appear to garner support among those disaffected from Duarte's policy failures and were criticized by prominent leaders. "[Salvadorans] have a political memory," editorialized Jesuits at the Central American University. "They know that certain more radical and violent actions can lead them again to the slaughterhouse without promising better times for their children." That the slaughter could begin again in El Salvador seemed inconceivable. Yet late in 1987 two prominent human rights activists, Herbert Anaya and René Cárdenas Vargas, were assassinated.

In March 1988 Salvadorans went again to the polls in legislative elections. And again they faced guerrilla attacks, road blocks, and power blackouts to do so. The results were a crushing defeat for Duarte and the Christian Democrats. The ARENA party, now headed by Alfredo Christiani, won a majority of the mayoralties, including the capital, San Salvador, and an absolute majority in the assembly. In commenting on the Christian Democrats' defeat, FDR President Guillermo Ungo explained that in a contest of robbers versus killers, the killers had won. Beyond the sarcasm of his remark, however, was the hard truth that rampant corruption at the highest levels and the failure of the Christian Democrats to deliver on their promises of welfare for the people had dramatically reversed their political fortunes.

While North American leaders praised the electoral process in El Salvador, other analysts worried about the political meaning of a reinvigorated right wing, capable, perhaps, of capturing the presidency in 1989. From the resurgence of death squad activities to the rise in mass demonstrations, signs were increasing that the democratic middle represented by Duarte and the Christian Democrats was fading. A new and more ferocious confrontation between left and right in El Salvador could present the United States again with the choices avoided at such high cost in 1980: increased repression, guerrilla victory, or a direct U.S. intervention.

KEY FACTS ABOUT EL SALVADOR:*

Population: 5,300,000; 43 percent urban

Area: 8,260 square miles, or about the size of Massachusetts

Infant Mortality (1985): 65 deaths per 1,000 live births during the course of the first year of life

Per Capita Income (GNP, 1985): US $820

Size of Armed Forces (includes total armed forces, does not include reserves or paramilitary): 47,000

Literacy: 72 percent

President and next scheduled election: José Napoléon Duarte was sworn in as president in June 1985. Alfredo Christiani of the Arena party was elected president in March 1989.

Total External Debt (in millions of dollars): US $1,736

Per Capita Military Spending: US $31

Honduras: The Cleanup Brigade

It is ironic that once-sleepy Honduras, the original "banana republic," should be at the center of the Central American conflict. The butt of jokes, its capital referred to as Teguci*golpe* because of the frequency of *golpes de estado,* or coups against the govern-

*Sources: see below, p. 90.

ment, Honduras became crucial to the support of U.S. policy in both El Salvador and Nicaragua in the 1980s.

Yet Honduras is a fragile base upon which to build such weighty policies. In 1981, the country held its first direct elections for president and Congress in over twenty-five years. Ending a decade of direct military rule, the elections may in retrospect mark the beginning of a transition to true civilian control, or they may represent a return to a civilian puppet government for the military that has been the customary form of Honduran politics for a generation. In November 1985, national elections for president and the legislature provided the first democratic transition from one civilian president to another in 50 years.

Like the rest of Central America, except Costa Rica, Honduras has been struggling to accommodate new political actors into a game dominated by traditional elites relying on the military to defend their privileges. But for unique historical reasons, the poor and disadvantaged in Honduras have been less strident in their demands on the system and the military more disposed to adopt modest reform to try to preempt social pressure before it became explosive. Honduras is also the last Central American country to retain working remnants of the nineteenth-century Liberal and Conservative (in Honduras, Nationalist) parties. Factionalized and elitist, the parties have, nevertheless, served to articulate public opinion and motivate voter participation. In the elections of 1981, a turnout of some 80 percent of registered voters cast over 90 percent of the ballots for either the Nationalists or the Liberals. Dr. Roberto Suázo Córdoba, a physician from Honduras's second city of San Pedro Sula, led the temporarily united factions of the Liberal party to a 52-to-40 percent defeat of the Nationalists.

By the mid-1980s Honduras's party system was beginning to show signs of breakdown. Rivalries within Suazo's Liberal party led to an extraconstitutional agreement to award the 1985 presidency to the leading candidate of the party that gained the most votes overall. The agreement was severely tested when the Liberals gained 49.2 percent of the overall vote (to the Nationalists' 43.9 percent), but their leading candidate, José Azcona Hoyo, only polled 27 percent of the vote compared to the Nationalists' candidate, Rafael Leonardo Callejas, who received more than 41 percent. The

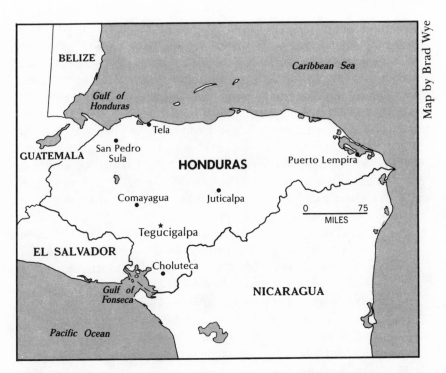

Map by Brad Wye

endorsement of the then-chief of the armed forces, General López Reyes, proved crucial to a resolution of the party dispute and the installation of Azcona as president in early 1986.

Analysts have viewed the victory of the Liberals over the Nationalists (traditionally backed by the military) in 1981 and 1985 as indicating popular skepticism about the value of the military's influence on politics. Yet since 1981 the military has repeatedly preserved its political prerogatives through the mechanism of its powerful policy-making group, the Supreme Council of the Armed Forces (CONSUFA). In the fall of 1983, then–commander in chief General Gustavo Alvarez Martínez signed an agreement with the United States to establish a Regional Military Training Center (CREM) for Hondurans and Salvadorans, then surrounded the capital with troops and announced the decision to the legislature and president. In March 1984, President Suazo and some junior officers pulled a surprise reverse coup on Alvarez and ousted him, apparently because of his disregard for customary collegial decision making in the armed forces and his close identification with U.S. interests in Honduras. The new commander in chief, General Walter López Reyes, while operating in a more traditional style for a Honduran commander and serving notice that the United States would have to compensate Honduras more generously for its support of U.S. strategic interests in the region, also made unilateral decisions about national policy and informed the president after the fact.

The key issue of U.S.-Honduran relations, for civilian and military circles alike, is Honduras's current role as the center of U.S. military operations in the region. Since 1980, Honduras has allowed anti-Sandinista forces (the contras), some 15,000 men, to operate out of its territory. Hondurans fear that a permanent cut in U.S. Congressional aid for the contras could leave a very destabilizing group of armed guerrillas inside the country. As the fortunes of the contras have risen and fallen with the U.S. Congress, the Honduran military has moved to restrict or expand the freedom of the contras to operate inside Honduras. Perhaps to deflect criticism of its own mounting human rights abuses, the army has documented alleged political murders and disappearances by the contras inside Honduras.

The U.S. Regional Military Training Center, established in 1983, was used to train Salvadoran and a much smaller number of Honduran troops in Honduras. The center could train Salvadorans at lower costs than would be entailed in transporting them to a U.S. facility, and it avoided the politically difficult alternative of raising the number of U.S. military trainers inside El Salvador, set at fifty-five by an understanding between Congress and the executive branch. Yet Honduras always considered El Salvador its primary regional adversary. El Salvador invaded Honduras in the 1969 "Soccer War," and the two countries have an unreconciled border dispute. In 1984, General López unilaterally suspended the use of the training center for Salvadorans, eventually closed it completely, and announced the need for a new security treaty between the United States and Honduras.

The United States has established a large military presence and substantial infrastructure in Honduras. U.S.-Honduran joint military exercises have occurred virtually nonstop since August 1983, involving up to 50,000 U.S. military personnel at a time. In addition, an undisclosed number of U.S. military officers fly intelligence reconnaissance missions over El Salvador and Nicaragua and assisted the contras in their war against the Sandinistas. The U.S. military's construction over the past two years has included hospitals, airports, listening stations, tank trenches, living quarters, and so on. The U.S. government denies that any of these facilities are permanent, but the Government Accounting Office (GAO) has criticized the program as stretching the definition of "temporary" to avoid the specific authorization from Congress that would be required for "permanent" facilities. Should the United States decide to undertake direct military action in Nicaragua, all the logistical preparations are in place in Honduras.

Resentment of the United States for its use of Honduras as a staging area grew. In late 1984, Honduras formally requested a better deal. Militarily, Honduras asked for revisions in the 1954 bilateral military assistance agreement to clarify the growing U.S. presence in Honduras, a separate bilateral security arrangement, and more training of Hondurans in the Regional Training Center. Four hundred million dollars in assistance over the next several years was requested to bolster the Honduran economy, which faces low prices for bananas and coffee, the region's lowest per capita income ($720), negative economic growth rates since 1982, and heavy expenditures for its contribution to the joint military exercises. Military aid, which was less than $4 million in 1980, has averaged over $64 million yearly since 1983. Special emergency military aid of $20 million was provided to Honduras in the wake of a Sandinista "incursion" into Honduran territory in 1986. In 1987 the Administration notified Congress of its intent to sell 10 F-5E fighter jets to Honduras over the next two years to maintain its air force as the best in Central America. In March 1988 more than 3,200 U.S. troops landed in Honduras in response to another Sandinista incursion apparently designed to destroy the contras' supply bases in Honduras. The total U.S. aid to Honduras (military and economic) in fiscal year 1987 was more than $250 million.

Hondurans are not united in their outlook on such close U.S.-Honduran security ties. Traditionally, Honduras harbored less animosity toward the United States than did Guatemala, El Salvador, or Nicaragua, despite the pervasiveness of North American culture and economy in the country since United Fruit first set up its headquarters there in 1909. Many feel that acting as a base of U.S. operations against Nicaragua can lead only to trouble; others argue that it is the best protection against the Sandinistas. Still others worry that the military emphasis of policy in the area strengthens the hand of the armed forces to the detriment of civilians in government, Honduras's uniquely vibrant trade unions, and its relatively free press.

Whatever complacency U.S. policymakers may have had about nationalist reactions to the U.S. presence was ended by Honduran reaction to the arrest of reputed drug kingpin Juan Ramón Matta Ballesteros, and his extradition to the United States in April 1988. Fifteen hundred demonstrators protested Matta's removal from Honduras and eventual extradition to the United States as a violation of the Honduran constitution. They attacked and burned the U.S. Embassy annex in Tegucigalpa and set fire to twenty of the embassy's vehicles. Four student demonstrators were shot, a fourteen-year-old burned to death, and some $6 million in damages was done to embassy property. While Honduran government officials blamed drug traffickers for inciting the riot that led to a declaration of emergency in the country, others believed the attack to be the result of simmering resentment of the U.S. presence and the heavy hand of U.S. officials on Honduran affairs.

KEY FACTS ABOUT HONDURAS:*

Population: 4,700,000: 39 percent urban

Area: 43,277 square miles, or slightly larger than Tennessee

Infant Mortality (1985): 76 deaths per 1,000 live births during the course of the first year of life

Per Capita Income (GNP, 1985): US $720

Size of Armed Forces (includes total armed forces, does not include reserves or paramilitary): 16,950

*Sources: see below, p. 90

Literacy: 59 percent

President and next scheduled election: José Simeon Azcona del Hoyo assumed office in January 1986. The next presidential election is scheduled for November 1989.

Total External Debt (in millions of dollars): US $2,713

Per Capita Military Spending: US $16

Costa Rica: "Our Weakness Is Our Defense"

The road to the town of Liberia is a pleasant one that winds its way through Costa Rica's lush central highlands, then drops down to the flat plains of this country's "Wild West." A trip through the verdant countryside tells one a great deal about Costa Rica. Modest homes of wood and cement dot the landscape. There is poverty to be sure, but little of the squalor that dominates much of rural Latin America. Schools appear at roadsides in population centers of any size and brilliant white clinics with neat red crosses are visible from time to time.

The metaphor for what makes Costa Rica different from the rest of Central America may well be the passing lanes of the country's major highways. Driving an automobile in Latin America is usually intimately connected with asserting one's manhood; risks are taken routinely to demonstrate that death can be challenged and beaten. How "un-Latin," then, of the Costa Ricans to provide safe passing on hills. Absent is the joy of pulling out from behind a belching bus to encounter another driver closing in at breakneck speed from the opposite direction. In Costa Rica, one is reduced to motoring calmly around the offending vehicle at the next appropriate passing zone.

Costa Rican politics has for decades provided a passing lane for political passions. Since 1948, free and open elections have offered a highly literate population a voice in national life. In that same year, a generation's worth of progressive social legislation was ratified, the standing army was abolished, and a civic culture favoring compromise and the peaceful settlement of disputes instituted. In Central America, Costa Rica is not merely unique, it is virtually miraculous.

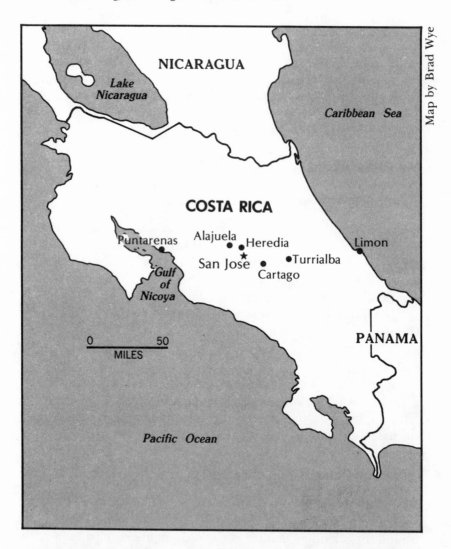

Back in Costa Rica's capital of San José, a Honduran and a North American visitor watch as the Costa Rican president and other politicians address a mildly enthusiastic crowd of schoolchildren who have been given the day off to celebrate Costa Rica's proclamation of neutrality. The speeches, although florid in the Latin style, are amazingly short. The entire rally lasts little more than an hour. As the president slowly descends from the podium, a boy and girl stand at his side guiding his steps. The president then walks among the crowd, virtually without security. The Honduran wonders aloud when his country will be able to achieve the political maturity of these Costa Ricans. The North American ponders his country's policies. Are they helping to preserve this precious outpost of democracy or, in the interest of broader regional objectives, do they risk sacrificing it to the chaos that consumes so much of Central America?

Costa Rica's contemporary political arrangements stem directly from the "revolution" of 1948. In the "revolution," a collection of anticommunist forces from different parts of the political spectrum combined to overthrow a coalition government of moderate conservatives, progressive forces in the Catholic Church, and a strong Communist party—a coalition that could only make sense in Latin America. Progressive social policies such as social security legislation and a strong income-tax law, and the increasing influence of Communists in the government, sparked opposition. But the immediate impetus for the revolt was the rigging of the elections of 1948 to maintain the government coalition in power. Protests over the election results mushroomed into armed conflict led by a successful landowner, José ("Pepe") Figueres Ferrer. His Forces of National Liberation, with assistance from a United States worried about Communist influence, defeated the standing army of the government and ushered in a new era of Costa Rican politics.

In victory, National Liberation set precedents of civility and compromise that would mark Costa Rican politics down to the present day. It abolished many unions and outlawed the Communist party, which had been particularly strong among organized banana workers. But it also instituted a major tax on wealth, eliminated the standing army, and extended full political rights to women and blacks. After ruling for an interim period, Figueres returned political power to the true victor of the 1948 election and formed his own political party, the National Liberation party (PLN), which adopted many of the progressive reforms of the prior coalition government as its own platform. Although elected to the presidency in 1953 (with "Don Pepe" as its candidate), the PLN has frequently turned over power to the opposition in electoral contests that have been largely free and fair. Under PLN leadership, the government's role in the economy grew through the nationalization of the country's bank, insurance, transportation, and utility industries, and the joint public-private financing of many productive enterprises. Other legislation enacted social welfare programs for medical care, social security, housing subsidies, and numerous other services to benefit the middle class and, to a lesser extent, the lower class.

The "revolution of 1948" helped Costa Rica avoid many of the political problems that affected the rest of Central America. But it could not eliminate the economic problems that afflicted all of the small Central American exporters in the late 1970s and 1980s. In the worldwide recession of the late 1970s, prices for Costa Rica's main exports, coffee and bananas, fell drastically, while expenditures for imported oil escalated. To cover the gap between earnings and expenditures and to maintain the country's politically popular consumer-goods imports, Costa Rica borrowed heavily on the international market. When international credit dried up in 1981–82, Costa Rica nearly went bankrupt. Austerity programs, international aid, rescheduled loans, and declining oil prices stabilized the country in the early 1980s, while Costa Rica sought longer-term solutions to its economic crisis.

As economic problems stabilized, due in part to increased U.S. aid ($128 million from 1977 to 1982; $973 million from 1983 to 1987), political problems multiplied. Real declines in most Costa Ricans' standard of living activated Costa Rica's unions and drove the rural poor into burgeoning squatter settlements around the major cities. Middle-class dissatisfaction with the elimination of government subsidies could no longer be bought off by a government strapped for operating funds.

Foreign-policy problems intruded ever more strongly into the already confused domestic scene. The continued radicalization of the Sandinista revolution polarized Costa Rican politics. In 1984 a Nicaraguan draft dodger was alleged to have been forcibly removed by Sandinista police from asylum in the Costa Rican Embassy in Managua. Costa Rican housewives marched on the presidential palace carrying pairs of trousers and demanded that President Luis Alberto Monge "put on his pants" and act tough by breaking diplomatic relations with Nicaragua and invoking the Río Treaty of mutual defense with the United States. Relations with Nicaragua reached their low point in May 1985 when Costa Rican border guards were fired on by Sandinista soldiers and two were killed. Despite President Monge's pledge of neutrality, U.S. officials worked to solidify a "southern front" in Costa Rica of clandestine airfields and other support facilities for the contras. Nicaragua in turn filed suit with the World Court against what Nicaragua charged was Costa Rican complicity in contra activities.

In the campaign leading up to the February 1986 presidential and Congressional elections, massive funding from the U.S. Republican party was alleged to be flowing to the National Liberation party's opposition, the PUSC (United Social Christian Party), which promised to move Costa Rica more closely to the U.S. position in Central America. The surprise victor, however, was Oscar Arias Sánchez, maintaining the National Liberation party in power. Arias moved aggressively to shut down contra activities in his country, at times coming under strong pressure from the United States. In March 1987 Costa Rica formally protested U.S. violation of Costa Rica's declared neutrality by continuing to use secret air bases ordered closed by Arias and by illegally funneling aid to contras operating on Costa Rican territory.

President Arias also sought to revive the moribund Central American peace process. To the surprise of most observers and the dismay of some, the five Central American presidents signed a modification of Arias's original peace plan in the town of Esquipulas, Guatemala on August 7, 1987. Suspect by the extreme left and right, the Guatemala plan opened up new political space in Central America and led to dramatic developments in many of the signatory countries, but most especially in Nicaragua.

Hailed by supporters of negotiated solutions to the region's conflicts and honored with the Nobel Peace Prize for 1987, Arias assumed new stature as a voice of compromise and conciliation. An end to the Central American wars is the principal requirement for Costa Rica to be able to address its pressing economic concerns. However, the investment of Arias's prestige and talent for negotiation in the peace process bears obvious risks as well if it is ultimately unsuccessful. By the time of the next scheduled elections in 1990, Costa Ricans will judge the president's party on what he has done to resolve the continuing economic pain this island of democracy is suffering.

CENTRAL AMERICAN PEACE PROPOSALS: A PERSPECTIVE FROM THE YEAR 2020

The process of regional negotiation and dialogue that began on the resort island of Contadora in 1983 and continued through the Arias Plan and the signing of the Esquipulas II accord on August 6, 1987 represented a turning point in Central America's development as a region of independent states in charge of their own destiny. Despite the persistence of fragile economies that make them vulnerable to outside forces beyond their control, Central American leaders in the late 1980s took into their own hands decisions about their future that had often by default been given to others. For this reason the Central American peace process in its various guises will be marked as a significant event, whether it ultimately produces peace or not.

In January 1983, representatives of four Latin American countries met on a resort island off the coast of Panama to discuss what they could do collectively about the Central American crisis. Mexico, Colombia, Panama, and Venezuela each had different perspectives on and relations with key countries in Central America, but all had a common interest in preventing unilateral action by the United States in the region and in seeking a negotiated solution to conflicts within and among the Central American countries.

Many who are unfamiliar with the nature of complex negotiation processes such as that undertaken by Contadora express frustration with the failure of the process to produce complete peace. Like all negotiations, Contadora accepted the role of achieving a balance among all the forces at work in Central America. That meant giving some concessions to the Sandinista government, its external opposition, the Duarte government and its guerrilla opposition, the fears of Nicaragua about the United States, and the fears of the United States and certain Central American countries about the Sandinistas. Contadora could make progress only to the degree that the parties to the conflicts in the region, principally the Central American countries and the United States, were willing to accept such concessions. From 1983 until 1987 Contadora foundered as different actors at different times and for different reasons were unwilling to concede ground to their adversaries.

The main stumbling block to concessions from 1984 to 1986 was the mutual suspicion and hostility between the United States and Nicaragua. Contadora, by its nature as a negotiation process, accepted the possibility of the continuation of the Sandinistas in power, while seeking to create agreements backed by international supervision that would protect the other Central American countries from Nicaragua and Nicaragua from the United States. When the Sandinistas agreed in whole or in part to draft treaties prepared by the Contadora ministers, the Reagan Administration took credit in a leaked National Security Council background paper for having "trumped the latest Nicaraguan-Mexican efforts to rush signature of an unsatisfactory Contadora agreement," and for having "effectively blocked Contadora group efforts to impose the second draft of the Revised Contadora Act." As it became clearer that the Reagan Administration would never trust any Sandinista government to fulfill treaty commitments and that the Sandinistas would not voluntarily surrender power, Contadora stalled.

A breakthrough came when Costa Rican President Oscar Arias unveiled his own peace plan on February 15, 1987. The genius of the Arias Plan (recognized by the awarding of the Nobel Peace Prize to President Arias) was to separate out the contentious security and enforcement provisions of Contadora and to proceed with political steps that gave parity to all the governments of the region. In their first meeting at the Central American religious shrine of Esquipulas in 1986 and then in Guatemala City in 1987, a kind of chemistry began to develop among the Central American presidents that facilitated mutual recognition.

The so-called Esquipulas II or Guatemala accords that resulted from the presidents' second meeting on August 6, 1987 included many of the points made in the Arias Plan. Their principal provisions were:

- to promote national reconciliation through internal political dialogue with unarmed opposition groups, a decree of amnesty for armed opposition groups and release of prisoners, and establishment of national reconciliation commissions to oversee amnesty, cease-fires, democratization, and free elections;

- to negotiate cease-fire agreements with armed opposition groups and to incorporate them into the existing "constitutional framework";

- to democratize political procedures through the granting of full freedom of speech, press, assembly, and political activity, and the ending of existing states of emergency;

- to appeal to all governments aiding armed rebels to cease such aid and to deny use of their territory to attack other states or to resupply armed groups; and

- to verify compliance with the agreements according to a strict timetable through an International Verification and Follow-up Commission of the secretaries general of the United Nations and the Organization of American States and the foreign ministers of Central America, the Contadora Group, and the Support Group of Argentina, Brazil, Peru, and Uruguay.

After years of stalemate, expectations rose rapidly with the signing of the accords. Concrete deeds followed dramatic announcements of cease-fires, expansions of political freedoms, and internal dialogue. As attention focused again on Nicaragua even critics of the Sandinistas were forced to admit by early 1988 that six months of negotiations had produced more concessions by Nicaragua than six years of the contra war.

The peace accords had an equally dramatic effect on developments in the United States. Congressional Democrats opposed to Administration policy finally had a concrete alternative to military aid to the contras. The next summit of the five presidents on January 15, 1988 issued a weak final communiqué that abolished the verification commission and merely called on the presidents to fulfill their remaining commitments "immediately, totally, and unconditionally" without setting any concrete timetable. But announcements by President Ortega that he would end the state of emergency and initiate direct talks with the contras helped to defeat a long-delayed request for military aid to the Nicaraguan opposition on February 3.

The ending of U.S. aid appeared to spur cease-fire talks between the Sandinistas and the contras. On March 23 at the border town of Sapoa, Nicaragua, a temporary cease-fire between the government and the "resistance" (as they were now called by the Sandinistas) appeared to promise an end to the years of bloody conflict. Almost immediately splits within the resistance emerged as its political wing sought to negotiate a return to political participation inside Nicaragua. With few fighters and all U.S. aid ended, their advantage lay in securing guarantees that would allow them to become a political opposition force that could meaningfully compete with the Sandinistas. The military wing pushed for concessions that would have broken the Sandinistas' primacy in the government and won for them at the negotiating table power that they had not won on the battlefield. As resistance demands escalated and their soldiers retreated to safe camps in Honduras, the talks stalled and then collapsed in June. Although the temporary cease-fire held throughout the summer, an attempted renewal of the talks in September failed to agree even on a site for the next meeting.

While world attention focused on Nicaragua, the peace accords also had their effect in El Salvador, Guatemala, and Honduras. President Duarte at first took advantage of the accords to press the case against the guerrillas. Just as President Ortega's position had been strengthened by the implicit recognition of his government by the other Central American presidents, so too Duarte could claim that the guerrillas had no standing unless they accepted his government as legitimate and laid down their arms. Nevertheless, civilian allies of the rebels took advantage of the political space created inside El Salvador to return and compete for office in the 1989 elections.

In Guatemala inconclusive talks with the guerrillas were held by the National Reconciliation Commission without great results and violence even escalated. Renewed drama came to the peace process in late November when the five Central American foreign ministers advanced a Honduran-authored plan to establish an international peacekeeping force to stop the provision of arms and territorial sanctuary to irregular armed forces.

By late 1988 the Central American peace process became the prisoner of internal political developments in Central America and the United States. Central America looked north for signs from an incoming Bush administration that it would develop a new U.S. approach to the region. Impending elections in El Salvador and Costa Rica drew political leaders' attention inward.

Critics of the Central American peace process have stressed its ambitious agenda, its lack of enforcement provisions, and its insensitivity to the security needs of the United States. These are reasons why this attempt to resolve peacefully the problems of decades may fail. But when the history of the 1980s and 1990s is written in the next century, the process will stand out as a significant confirmation of the emergence of Latin America as a mature actor on the international stage.

KEY FACTS ABOUT COSTA RICA:*

Population: 2,800,000: 45 percent urban

Area: 19,575 square miles, or smaller than West Virginia

Infant Mortality (1985): 19 deaths per 1,000 live births during the course of the first year of life

Per Capita Income (GNP, 1985): US $1,300

Size of Armed Forces (includes civil and rural guard only): 9,500

Literacy: 94 percent.

*Sources: see below, p. 90

President and next scheduled election: Licenciado Oscar Arias Sánchez took office in May 1986. The next presidential election is scheduled for February 1990.

Total External Debt (in millions of dollars): US $4,191

Per Capita Military Spending: US $0

Guatemala: All the Democracy That Fits

Nearly 5,000 Guatemalans have been seized without warrant and killed since General Lucas García became President of Guatemala in 1978. The bodies of the victims have been found piled up in ravines, dumped at roadsides or buried in mass graves. Thousands bore the scars of torture, and death had come to most by strangling with a garrotte, by being suffocated in rubber hoods or by being shot in the head.

—Amnesty International, *Guatemala: A Government Program of Political Murder* (London), February 1981.

Political violence rose sharply during October and November, surpassing almost every previous month since [civilian] President Cerezo took office [in 1986]. "Disappearance" and kidnapping statistics for these months paralleled those under past military regimes (37 during October and 43 in November) while killings increased as well; according to the press, less than one-third were attributable to common crime. . . . Archbishop Próspero Penados del Barrio told Americas Watch, "The military hasn't changed at all. [President] Vinicio [Cerezo] can't do anything."

—Americas Watch Committee, *Guatemala News in Brief,* October/November 1987.

The record of Guatemalan politics since the CIA-engineered coup that overthrew the elected government of Colonel Jacobo Arbenz in 1954 should give pause to those who believe that democracy can be installed in Central America by armed force. From that date military government followed military government (with some brief civilian interludes); coups or rigged elections were the routine means of changing national leaders; and a guerrilla movement founded by young, reformist military officers grew during the 1960s. With the inauguration of civilian President Vinicio Cerezo in 1986 Guatemala's hopes for democracy were raised again.

Guatemala stands apart from its sister countries for more than the dubious distinction of having the most violent contemporary history of any of the bloodstained nations of Central America. More U.S. companies have branches or subsidiaries in Guatemala than

Map by Brad Wye

in any other Central American nation. Guatemala has rich oil deposits. Its population is the largest on the isthmus, and, unique to Guatemala among the Central American countries, 50 percent of its people are pure-blood Indians who maintain a life-style close to that of their Mayan forebears. The beauty of Guatemala's people, culture, and countryside has been surpassed, unfortunately, only by the brutality of its decades-old civil strife.

The fraudulent election of General Romeo Lucas García in March 1978 ushered in a new period of extreme repression of political liberties and of human rights abuses. The guerrilla movement, supposedly crushed in the 1960s, reappeared and threatened for the first time to forge links to Guatemala's majority Indian population. Lucas's ultraconservative military government instituted a "scorched-earth" policy against the guerrillas and the Indians. Those suspected of sympathizing with the guerrillas were massacred, and their villages, crops, and livestock destroyed. Guatemala had lost U.S. economic and military assistance in 1977 when it refused to meet President Jimmy Carter's human rights requirements for aid. With political deaths averaging some 600 a month throughout the late 1970s and early 1980s, Guatemala became an international pariah. Oblivious to world opinion, Guatemala preferred to fight its insurgency ruthlessly without the external restraints that would accompany foreign aid.

In March 1982, another rigged election brought Lucas García's hand-picked candidate, General Angel Aníbal Guevara, into the presidential office. Charges of fraud by the political parties were rampant, and much of the military opposed continuation of the Lucas García–style government. Seventeen days after the election, six junior military officers led a bloodless coup to prevent Guevara's inauguration. They called upon retired General Efraín Ríos Montt—their former instructor at the military college—to head a new military government.

Ríos Montt, an evangelical Christian in predominantly Catholic Guatemala, was portrayed initially as a reformer concerned about human rights. However, his government continued the crackdown on political activists, guerrillas, and Indians. A civic-action program to ensure the allegiance of the Indians was developed. Ríos Montt's so-called "Beans and Rifles" strategy involved organizing Indians into civil-defense patrols in return for access to food and health care. Under the watchful eye of the military, Indian men and boys went out on patrols to fight the guerrillas. The ability of the military to keep tight surveillance and control over vast rural areas through this network of patrols led one human rights group to call Guatemala a "nation of prisoners." Once again the guerrilla threat seemed to have been beaten back.

But dissatisfaction within the military's ranks prompted a coup against Ríos Montt in August 1983. It was carried out by the high command which, under the leadership of General Oscar Humberto Mejía Víctores, had reacted to Ríos Montt's managerial incompetence, to his infusion of religion into political and military matters, and to the international isolation of Guatemala.

General Mejía Víctores remained commander in chief of the Guatemalan armed forces, and the de facto head of state, until the elections of November 1985. He governed by decree, after conferring with a group of military advisers. Despite the apparent destruction of the guerrilla forces, the Mejía Víctores government remained preoccupied with a possible resumption of the insurgency. Consequently, the government concentrated on denying the guerrillas support by incorporating the Indians into national life through participation in civil-defense forces and resettlement to so-called model villages, and on improving Guatemala's chances to obtain international economic and military assistance. Deaths attributable to human rights abuses declined to an average of 90 per month in 1985, and some opening of the political system began under his rule.

General Mejía moved to improve the domestic climate and to foster better relations with the United States and with the rest of Latin America by holding elections to a Constituent Assembly in July 1984, the first elections without substantial fraud since 1954. The Constituent Assembly was charged with framing a new constitution and overseeing presidential elections set for November 1985.

In the presidential elections of 1985, a crowded field of candidates ranging ideologically from the center to the extreme right competed in a first round in November. When none obtained an absolute majority, a runoff was held that pitted centrist Christian Democrat Marco Vinicio Cerezo Arévalo against center-right newspaper magnate Jorge Carpio Nicolle. Although accused of being a leftist by Carpio, Cerezo was careful to avoid any mention of land reform in his campaign, and to deny that he would investigate the army for political assassinations and disappearances. In the December runoff Cerezo won 68 percent of the vote to 32 percent for his opponent.

Vinicio, as he was always referred to by affectionate supporters, began his new administration with a "honeymoon" of international and domestic goodwill. Yet the new president understood the restraints on his rule. In an interview in *Time* magazine before his electoral victory he stated, "In the first six months I'll have 30 percent of the power. In the first two years I'll have 50 percent, and I'll never have more than 70 percent of the power during my five-year term." Guatemalan Archbishop Penados was even less sanguine, estimating that a civilian ruler would never have more than 20 percent of the power.

The reasons for military tolerance of a return to civilian rule are complex. As the new administration quickly found out, the military had paid for their counterinsurgency war and the requisite graft during the long aid cutoff by stripping every social program bare. The cost of "defending the fatherland" was a massive "social debt" of mounting infant mortality, increasing hunger, and a decaying infrastructure of schools, highways, and public services. This burden would be more easily borne, the military reasoned, by a country under civilian rule.

Some in the armed forces recognized as well that the cycle of violence and repression would continue unless certain changes were allowed. After the 1976 earthquake that had devastated Guatemala's countryside, elements of the military had begun to conclude that some organizing of the rural population was essential if only on grounds of "national security." Triumphant about their achievements in defeating the insurgency yet again, the Guatemalan army could afford the luxury of civilian participation and even benefit from an improved international image and the possible resumption of economic and military aid.

Vinicio has been careful to keep his end of the bargain. Despite pressure from local and international advocacy groups, he has kept his campaign promises of not investigating the military for their past (and current) abuses and avoiding the dreaded issue of land reform. While killings and "disappearances" continue, political spaces have opened to permit the return of some political exiles. Political parties are allowed to operate and the outlawed peasant organization, Committee of Campesino Unity (CUC), has been permitted to apply for legal status. Trade union activity has grown, with workers in the public and private sectors striking regularly. In March 1988 the president signed an accord with the country's trade unions that calls for a restoration of price controls on staple items and the institution of a minimum wage.

These measures, while seen as advancements by working people, have met with disapproval from the nation's business and agricultural sectors. These sectors were equally dismayed by Congressional passage of a new income tax law. Some say the military instigated the new law, which leans heavily on the middle and upper classes, to share the burden of running the state. In May, officers from a traditionally conservative area of Guatemala led an abortive coup against the government. As 1988 ended coup rumors swirled around the Cerezo government, while it became even more dependent on Defense Minister Gramajo and other officers who were committed to maintaining civilian rule.

The president has been successful in renegotiating much of Guatemala's foreign debt, and has drawn new or increased foreign aid from many countries including the United States, Taiwan, West Germany, France, Mexico, and Spain. The national currency, the quetzal, has stabilized, and inflation has been reduced by some 30 percent. After five years of negative growth, modest growth has been restored to the national economy.

Vinicio Cerezo's presidency has brought change to Guatemala, but that change is not yet profound. He has not significantly improved the lives of the poor majority nor has he abated the country's endemic political violence. Some of his policies have stirred the ire of the wealthy elite, but more important to his remaining in office, he has worked well within the boundaries acceptable to the military. History will judge Vinicio Cerezo favorably if he is able to translate the popular support that exists for him personally into institutional legitimacy for civilian rule.

KEY FACTS ABOUT GUATEMALA:*

Population: 8,400,000: 41 percent urban

Area: 42,042 square miles, or the size of Tennessee

*Sources: See below, p. 90.

Infant Mortality (1985): 65 deaths per 1,000 live births during the course of the first year of life

Per Capital Income (GNP, 1985): US $1,250

Size of Armed Forces (includes total armed forces, does not include reserves or paramilitary): 40,200

Literacy: 55 percent

President and next scheduled election: Marco Vinicio Cerezo Arévalo took office in January 1986. The next scheduled presidential election is September 1990.

Total External Debt (in millions of dollars): US $2,595

Per Capita Military Spending: US $21

Sources for Key Facts

Area: *World Almanac, 1988*
Infant Mortality, Per Capita Income, and Total External Debt: International Bank for Reconstruction and Development, *World Development Report 1987.*
Size of Armed Forces: International Institute for Strategic Studies, *The Military Balance 1986–1987.*
Literacy, Military Spending, and Population: John W. Sewell and Stuart K. Tucker, eds., *Agenda 88: Growth, Exports, and Jobs in a Changing World Economy* (New Brunswick, N.J.: Transaction Books, 1988)
Election information source: Provided by the individual Central American embassies in the United States.

3

Five Countries and Ten Questions: The Policy Debate

President John F. Kennedy is said to have remarked about Washington, D.C., that it combined northern charm and southern efficiency: neither attractive nor a good place to get much done. Perhaps he would have modified his harsh words if he had lived to the 1980s, when many American cities were in decline and Washington continued to expand, added one of the most beautiful subway systems in the world, and became much more cosmopolitan.

But it is curious how Washington both attracts and repels its citizens. Since 1976, it has been in vogue for national politicians to run against Washington. According to these politicians, Washington, as the symbol of the Federal Government, is to be blamed for what is wrong in voters' lives. The home of "big government," Washington regulates, restricts, interferes, requires, legislates, overspends, and, above all, overtaxes a citizenry which, if left to its own devices, could achieve a more harmonious union. Being against Washington and the evil deeds done there is to be on the side of all that has made America great.

Yet many of those who come to Washington to do the nation's business contract "Potomac fever," a fascination with the power and prestige that emanate from Washington, and never want to

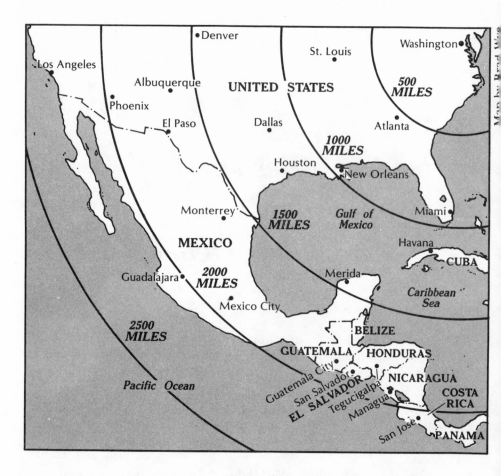

"*San Salvador is closer to Houston, Texas, than Houston is to Washington, D.C.*"

—President Ronald Reagan, May 1984

leave. Potomac fever affects not only senators, congressmen, presidents, and cabinet officers, but also their staffs and the panoply of policy analysts, "think-tankers," lobbyists, public relations experts, and others who earn their living from, and bask in the reflected glory of, the fact that decisions affecting the nation's and the world's future are made "inside the Beltway."

To understand policy debates in Washington, it is helpful to know something about what shapes the attitudes and behavior of those who make policy and those who make it their business to develop an alternative, "better" policy than the one being followed. Stereotypical portraits of two types of people who make and unmake policy in Washington are presented below. The national security analyst and the human rights activist rarely exist in the form in which they are presented here and do not exhaust the range of policy types. But as ideal types they are especially relevant for a discussion of U.S. policy toward Central America.

There are many ways in which North Americans are divided over Central America. The division between those concerned primarily about the advancement of U.S. interests in the world and strategic threats to these interests from Central America, and those focused on the promotion and protection of Central Americans' human condition is among the most basic. Our purpose in stereotyping a fictitious national security analyst and a human rights activist is not to criticize either, but to illustrate the ways in which their basic assumptions cause them to talk past each other rather than to engage in constructive dialogue.

The National Security Analyst

"National security" is not a phrase that enters into the everyday language of most people. But it is the subject with the highest priority in Washington. It covers a range of activities that are thought necessary to preserve the American way of life, from the obvious requirements of defending the national territory to the promotion of U.S. prestige and the protection of American interests in various parts of the world. The definition of U.S. interests, and of which ones are more vital than others, is the job of the national security analyst in or out of government. As we will see, defining our interests in Central America is the most contested aspect of U.S. policy toward the region.

The national security analyst (or NSA) shares a set of assumptions with his or her colleagues. In the eyes of the NSA, defending the well-being of the United States is the highest duty any citizen can have and the greatest good. The protection of a country that stands for democracy, freedom, and prosperity is by its very nature a highly moral task.

The rub comes from the fact that the defense of the United States takes place in an amoral world. Nation-states, for the several hundred years they have existed, have engaged in the most heinous activities to protect themselves and to promote their own values. They are the foremost practitioners of the view that the end justifies the means. Among the means employed by nation-states in the recent past have been genocide, sabotage, political assassination, and the bombing of civilian populations with conventional, chemical, and nuclear explosives.

It is not surprising that, operating in the nasty world of nation-states, the NSA becomes cynical about the good that can be achieved in one's lifetime and impressed with humankind's capacity for evil. In this world of nation-states, the defense of the United States by means that in another context might seem suspect becomes acceptable and moral. The "real" world in which NSAs operate may require actions that would not normally be considered good or justifiable.

Human rights and democracy in other countries are an important concern for NSAs. But NSAs see a militarily strong United States that is able to prevail over its principal rival, the Soviet Union, as the main guarantor of all people's human rights. U.S. policies that result in victories for forces aligned with the Soviet Union do not protect human rights, but undermine them. Therefore, the United States may at times find itself in a strategic alliance with unsavory governments, not because it approves of their policies, but because of the assistance such a government may provide in the ultimate struggle against Soviet imperialism.

The relevance of this discussion to Central America is that the region has been defined by President Reagan and others as involving a vital interest of the United States—one for which citizens must be prepared to fight and die. So defined, Central America

DEFINING U.S. NATIONAL "INTERESTS"

The 167 countries of the world, whatever the nature of their economic or political systems, share the common foreign policy goal of protecting their "interests." "National interests" are those principles, beliefs, possessions, and practices that a nation will make commitments and sacrifices of varying intensity, short of war, to defend. "Vital interests" are those to which a nation will commit the maximum political, economic, and military resources.

A country's size, resources, location, and form of government help to determine how broadly its "interests" are defined. Small or weak powers may not be able even to defend their "vital interests" of protecting the national territory. Slightly larger, more powerful nations, such as Switzerland, may be willing to go to war only to repel attacks on their homeland and can be said to have few "interests" beyond their borders.

Great powers, or formerly great powers, define their interests more grandly. Britain, for example, was willing to go to war with Argentina to defend a few hundred British subjects on a small, barren island called the Falklands/Malvinas, located four thousand miles from England, near Antarctica.

The United States, the world's first superpower, endowed with enormous resources, has defined its interests more and more broadly since the Second World War. At various times it has viewed developments in any part of the world that diminished U.S. power or prestige as bearing on its national interests. The U.S. prime objective has been to prevent its strategic adversary, the Soviet Union, from dominating more countries than those over which it held sway at the end of the Second World War. To prevent the "loss" of countries to communism and to counter a presumed threat to its vital interests, the United States went to war in Korea (and won) and in Vietnam (and lost).

Since the promulgation of the Monroe Doctrine in 1823, the Caribbean Basin has been a special security interest of the United States. But after the last great imperial power, Britain, ended its presence in that region in the early twentieth century, the United States had no rivals in what came to be seen as its "sphere of influence." No threats to U.S. vital interests were seen as coming from the Caribbean Basin, and strategic priorities were focused elsewhere, primarily on the defense of Western Europe and Japan.

Now the creation of a Soviet ally in the region, Cuba, and developments in Grenada and Central America have raised security concerns for the United States in the Caribbean Basin. The classified U.S. Defense

Guidance, the definitive statement of U.S. security interests around the world, ranks the defense of the Caribbean Basin (including Central America) on a par with the continental United States.

> The primary objective is to maintain the security of the North American Continent, the contiguous Caribbean Basin, and the sea and air approaches thereto (including Hawaii. . . .)

> [This section of the U.S. Defense Guidance was declassified for use in a paper by Colonel Nestor G. Pino-María, "The Strategic Importance of Central America for the United States," (Washington, D.C.: Washington Institute for Values in Public Policy, 1985).]

On the basis of this U.S. Defense Guidance, hostile developments in Central America would be defined as threatening "vital interests" of the United States.

As a result of the Vietnam conflict, domestic consensus about the definition of U.S. vital interests has broken down. HRAs argue that Vietnam demonstrated that the United States cannot and need not try to control events everywhere in the Third World. In an international system in which it is no longer the uniquely dominant power it once was, the United States must, HRAs believe, define its interests more modestly, husbanding scarce resources and uncertain public support for those crucial issues that can affect the well-being of its citizenry. The emergence of leftist regimes in the tiny countries of Central America is not, in the view of HRAs, such a crucial issue.

NSAs believe that the United States lacks only the political will to become the preeminent power it once was. The international system, they believe, requires one unifying, ordering power, and no country except the United States can play that role. As the ordering power, the United States must demonstrate its ability to control developments across the globe and, especially, in its strategic "backyard" of Central America.

These competing visions of U.S. "vital interests" are at the heart of disputes over U.S. policy toward Central America.

becomes for the NSA an area in which the end (defense of vital U.S. interests) justifies an extensive list of means (overthrowing governments, mining harbors, waging guerrilla warfare, collaborating with drug dealers, and so on). If what happens in Central America is a vital interest of the United States, the "options list" of the NSA is limited basically by what the United States has the means to do, can gain the support of the public for, or can keep hidden from public view.

If you are made uncomfortable by the moral dilemmas inherent in the preceding paragraphs, you are not cut out to be an NSA.

The Human Rights Activist

Somewhere on a different part of the political spectrum, another type of policy person can be found. Human rights activists (HRAs) have been involved in policy debates for far less time than NSAs. Their emergence roughly corresponds to the breakdown during the Vietnam years of the foreign policy consensus that had endured since the Second World War. They, too, share certain assumptions about the way the world works and the role of U.S. policy in it.

A majority of the governments around the world, especially in the Third World and in the socialist bloc, engage in systematic violations of human rights through physical and mental torture, illegal detention, and prosecution; restriction of the rights of speech, assembly, association, and mobility; and other means. The HRA believes that the United States has an enviable, though imperfect, record of honoring human rights within its own borders and desires to extend those attitudes and practices to the rest of the world.

The HRA also believes, unlike the NSA, that the foreign policy of the United States should be formulated largely on the basis of respect for human rights. If other countries act in morally reprehensible ways by denying human rights, the best response of the United States is to denounce these abuses publicly and adopt policies designed to promote a climate of human rights protection. The United States should hold out its behavior, based on respect for persons and for the principle of law, as the example that others should follow. The United States should virtually never look the other way or support governments that violate human rights without making a major issue of those violations. In the long run, HRAs argue, principled behavior, based on human rights as the cornerstone of U.S. foreign policy, will do the most to protect U.S. national security by encouraging more equitable, responsive governments and, hence, a more peaceful world.

If a foreign policy determined largely by human rights considerations appears a bit naive to you, then you are not cut out to be an HRA.

NSAs and HRAs: The Difficult Dialogue

NSAs are usually in power in Washington and HRAs out of power, but not always. During the Carter Administration many HRAs, or those substantially agreeing with the HRAs' perspectives on the world, were in positions of power. They frequently clashed with NSAs in other parts of the administration and in the career bureaucracy who did not share the same assumptions about the conduct of U.S. foreign policy. This made for the worst of both worlds: HRAs announced new policies, NSAs stalled on implementing them, and the rest of the world became confused. The Iranian hostage crisis and the Soviet invasion of Afghanistan intervened to resolve this incongruity by making the world look so nasty that NSAs were put back in the saddle again. With the advent of the Reagan Administration, the HRAs returned to their customary positions outside of power. What influence they exercised then was largely through the pressure they could mobilize on Congress.

What follows are two questions about each of the five critical countries in Central America that figure in U.S. policy debates. Each question is answered from the point of view of our stereotypical policy types, the National Security Analyst (NSA) and the Human Rights Activist (HRA). As you weave your way through the debate try to determine for yourself which assumptions, predictions, and prescriptions make the most sense to you.

Nicaragua

Question: Is the Sandinista Regime in Nicaragua a Threat to U.S. Interests in Central America?

Discussion:

It is less than obvious to most North Americans how Nicaragua, a poor nation of just over three million people, could be a threat to a superpower like the United States. But for NSAs, Nicaragua under Sandinista control represents a clear threat to the security of the region, to U.S. interests in the area, and, ultimately, to the national security of the United States itself.

The first way in which NSAs consider Nicaragua a threat to U.S. interests is the obvious case in which Nicaragua becomes a base for Soviet strategic forces—bombers or missiles that could attack the United States. The Soviet Union and the United States came to the brink of nuclear war when the Soviets attempted to place intermediate-range nuclear missiles in Cuba in 1962. In response, the Kennedy administration imposed a blockade of Cuba until Soviet leader Nikita Khrushchev agreed to the removal of the missiles. Kennedy, in turn, pledged not to invade Cuba.

The United States has made it clear several times since 1962 that it will not tolerate the introduction of land-based strategic weapons into the hemisphere, and it is hard to imagine a rational Soviet leadership that would attempt such a step again. If it were to be tried, this would clearly constitute a change in the strategic position of the superpowers and be considered a vital threat to the United States. Of course, with its missile-bearing submarines (which are serviced in Cuba) stationed off the coasts of the United States, the Soviet Union already has nuclear warheads closer to our borders than basing in Nicaragua would provide. However, the addition of land-based missiles or bombers in Nicaragua would be a dramatic escalation of the Soviet presence in the area and, in the minds of most North Americans, constitute a threat to our vital interests.

The "MIG scare" at the end of 1984 raised a second way in which Nicaragua could be viewed as a threat to the vital interests of the United States. MIG-21s, more modern aircraft than those possessed by other Central American countries, were thought to be on their way to Nicaragua aboard Soviet ships. Not a direct threat to U.S. territory, the aircraft could nevertheless change the regional balance of power between Nicaragua and her neighbors, particularly Honduras and Costa Rica. If Nicaragua were to attack her neighbors, the United States and other Latin American countries would be obligated by the 1947 Río treaty of mutual assistance to come to the aid of the country under attack.

NSAs also view the MIGs as a more direct threat to the Caribbean waterways, called strategic lanes of communications (or SLOCs), through which 45 percent of U.S. foreign trade is shipped, 55 percent of U.S. crude oil imports pass, and 60 percent of supplies and reinforcements for a war in Europe or the Middle East would flow. The stationing of attack aircraft in Nicaragua would complement even more advanced planes already in Cuba and pose a potential threat to U.S. shipping in the event of certain kinds of limited conventional warfare. This is a situation which any reasonable military/strategic planner would like to avoid.

You may wonder how a nuclear superpower could be militarily preoccupied about attacks from small states in Central America and the Caribbean. Certainly war with the United States would be virtual suicide for the governments of Nicaragua or Cuba.

But NSAs are concerned about keeping as many options open as possible. Traditionally, the Caribbean Basin has been an area about which the United States did not need to be militarily concerned. This left military strategists free to allocate resources to other parts of the globe. The NSA sees a possibly hostile Nicaragua, linked to a small but tough Cuba (and, at one point, Grenada as well), as tying down the United States in an area that previously was of little concern to the military strategist. In their publication *The Soviet-Cuban Connection in Central America and the Caribbean* (March 1985), the Departments of State and Defense argued the issue this way:

> The Soviet Union sees in the region an excellent and low-cost opportunity to preoccupy the United States—the "main adversary" of Soviet strategy—thus gaining greater freedom of action for the Soviet Union. While the Soviets are not likely to mount a direct military challenge to the United States in the Caribbean Basin, they are attempting to foment as much unrest as possible in an area that is at the strategic crossroads of the Western Hemisphere. Working through its key proxy in the region, Cuba, the Soviet Union hopes to force the United States to direct attention and military resources to an area that has not been a serious security concern to the United States in the past. (p. 2.)

For the NSA, the mere possession of advanced fighter craft or perhaps other weapons that could be considered offensive rather than defensive is a threat to the interests of the United States.

The last way in which Nicaragua could be a threat to the United States is by its very nature as a so-called Marxist-Leninist state. There is still a debate among well-informed people about whether the predominance of Marxist-Leninists in the Sandinista government and their increasing alignment with Cuba and the Soviet Union puts Nicaragua in the category of states such as Cuba or countries in the Eastern bloc. And regardless of what eventually happens in Nicaragua, analysts will argue about whether policies of the present or previous administrations pushed Nicaragua unnecessarily in the direction of the Soviet camp. But for many,

Nicaragua is already a Marxist-Leninist state in the Soviet orbit and, by its nature, constitutes a threat to U.S. interests.

The reason is that Marxism-Leninism is said to be intrinsically expansionist and hence a threat to its neighbors either directly through attack or indirectly through subversion. Even if it never acquired a single MIG or installed Soviet missiles, Nicaragua would, according to this argument, constitute a threat to U.S. interests because of its desire to export revolution throughout the hemisphere.

This, of course, is the "domino theory" of Vietnam-era fame applied to Central America. In Central America, the domino theory works like this: Nicaragua becomes or already is a Marxist-Leninist state; little Nicaragua is not a threat to the United States, but Marxist-Leninist states are inherently expansionist and will subvert their neighbors, some of whom may fall to Marxism-Leninism themselves. A Marxist-Leninist Central America is a threat to more important countries in South America or to Mexico, a major supplier of oil to the United States that shares a two-thousand-mile border with us. Trouble in a border country like Mexico will eventually spill over into the United States in the form of migrants, terrorism, and the diversion of U.S. military force to defend a previously peaceful border. In other words, the domino theory says, today it may be Managua, but tomorrow Mexico City and the next day El Paso or Los Angeles.

From the perspective of the domino theory, the United States needs to be concerned about the character of regimes in Central America and to impose limits—by diplomacy if possible, by force if necessary—on what it considers to be acceptable governments in the region. Small countries such as those in Central America or even larger ones such as Mexico or Venezuela do not have the option of imposing limits on their neighbors, but the United States does. And in the nasty world of global power rivalries, NSAs argue, the United States needs to exercise that option to defend its own interests.

NSAs believe that U.S. responses to challenges in the Caribbean Basin will have a powerful impact on how other nations, particularly our allies and the Soviet Union, view the resolve of the United States. NSAs fear that if we are either unable or unwilling to control events close to home, our allies in Western Europe and the Third World will question our commitment to them. Furthermore, if the Soviet Union receives the message that the United States will not deter Soviet advances in a region so close to our borders, it may be tempted to test the United States in other parts of the world.

In discussing the ways in which Nicaragua could be seen as a threat to U.S. interests in Central America, we have gone from the fairly clear-cut case of potential strategic threat from nuclear weapons to the much more murky threat posed by the "domino theory." Among experts and the general public, support for U.S. military action to defend our perceived interests roughly parallels the nature of the threat: there is great consensus about the correctness of the use of force to prevent the installation of missiles, for example; much less about using force to change the character of a regime.

HRAs who criticize U.S. hostility toward Nicaragua are often astounded at how exercised the leaders of the most powerful country in the world are about a poor nation of less than three million people such as Nicaragua. Some accuse the United States of formulating foreign policy on the basis of a national *insecurity* that the United States is experiencing as Central America pursues a more independent course.

Like NSAs, HRAs draw a line at the introduction of strategic nuclear weapons into Central America by an outside power. They would seek to prevent such a development by making a clear public statement to the Soviet Union that land-based nuclear weapons would not be tolerated in the hemisphere. An accommodation with Nicaragua that would remove fear of the United States as a motivation or pretext for military steps on the part of the Sandinistas would also be sought.

HRAs tend to focus on the ways in which the United States is a threat to Nicaragua and explain the military buildup that has occurred as being a response to U.S. hostility. While NSAs talk about MIGs, and Hind-24 attack helicopters, HRAs criticize U.S. support for the contras as illegal, immoral, and counterproductive. They believe it has forced the Sandinistas to put more emphasis on military preparedness than would otherwise be the case. When NSAs point out that Nicaragua's buildup began before serious contra activities had been initiated, HRAs argue that, given the historical record, any revolutionary regime such as the Sandinistas has to anticipate a hostile U.S. response at some point. Some military preparation is necessary to raise the costs of a possible U.S. intervention. To the extent the HRAs accept that the United States has legitimate security concerns about military developments in Nicaragua, they believe that these should be dealt with through negotiation, not threats and intimidation.

The issue over which HRAs become the most outraged is the "domino theory." They deny that the emergence of communist regimes in Laos and Cambodia after the fall of South Vietnam confirms a domino theory. Revolution, as the product of particular political, economic, and social factors, cannot be exported to other countries, they argue.

The United States, HRAs note, has been particularly unable to predict which Latin American revolutions would be friends and which enemies of the United States. In Cuba, the Republican Eisenhower administration initially failed to oppose Fidel Castro who once in power became Moscow's greatest ally in the Western Hemisphere. In Mexico, the United States denounced the Mexican Revolution as a Bolshevik plot and intervened militarily to affect its outcome. Until the 1940s the United States railed against Mexican radicalism. Yet President Franklin Roosevelt's decision to ignore demands for reprisals against Mexico's nationalization of U.S. oil companies in the thirties and to reach an accommodation with Mexico helped to produce a stable and moderate Mexico and healthy U.S.-Mexican relations.

As a superpower, HRAs argue, the United States should become more relaxed about developments in its border region. It should promote policies to correct the poverty, hunger, disease, and inequality that foment revolution in Central America, make clear its unwillingness to allow outside powers such as the Soviet Union (or Cuba) to intervene, but let the power of U.S. markets, financial aid, cultural appeal, and democratic practices work its charm on regimes bent on rapid social change.

HRAs hesitate to call Nicaragua a communist regime. They recognize that there are dedicated Marxist-Leninists in the government. Yet they find the regime remarkably open a decade after the Sandinistas came to power compared to Cuba only two years after its revolution or, indeed, compared to noncommunist, authoritarian regimes in other parts of Central and Latin America to which the United States is much less hostile.

But HRAs also believe that Nicaragua has a right to any type of regime its people choose, even Marxist-Leninist. Just as a radical Nicaragua should be prevented from intervening in the affairs of its neighbors, so too the United States must refrain from attempting to impose its preferred system, democratic or not, on the Nicaraguans.

NSAs don't believe that a Marxist-Leninist regime is ever freely chosen but rather that it is imposed on an unwilling population. HRAs are not so sure. They view the obvious popularity of the Sandinistas after their triumph in 1979 as confirmation of the legitimacy of the government. They emphasize the health-care, literacy, and land-reform programs enacted during the early years of the Sandinista government as evidence of commitments to the common people of the country. The much disputed election of 1984, while flawed, is taken by HRAs as further confirmation of Sandinista legitimacy and commitment to some forms of political dissent. As with elections in other Latin countries, notably El Salvador, elections including a broader spectrum of political views could be imagined. For HRAs, new elections in Nicaragua might be desirable as part of some future political accord, but the 1984 Nicaraguan elections should not be condemned as totally fraudulent.

NSAs counter each one of these conclusions by HRAs. Their specific rejoinders can be found in a series of documents and analyses published by the State Department's Office of Public Diplomacy for Latin America and the Caribbean.[1] But the bottom line for NSAs is that the leaders of Nicaragua are Marxist-Leninists who will do or say anything to achieve their ultimate objective: domination of Nicaragua by a single party and alignment with Cuba and the Soviet Union. With this as their objective, there is little that the United States can do through negotiations or greater understanding to change Nicaragua's course. By its very nature, the NSAs say, a Sandinista Nicaragua constitutes a threat to the United States which must be faced.

Question: Does a Policy of Military and Economic Pressure on Nicaragua Have the Best Chance of Influencing the Sandinistas to Become More Democratic and Less Menacing to their Neighbors?

Discussion:

NSAs point to statements by the Sandinistas that are said to betray them as dedicated Marxist-Leninists who, by definition, will never accept true democracy. They cite a secret speech made in the spring of 1984 to the Nicaraguan Socialist Party (PSN), a Moscow-line communist party, by Sandinista National Directorate member and political coordinator Bayardo Arce acknowledging that the FSLN (Sandinista National Liberation Front) had never intended to carry out its promises to promote pluralism, a mixed economy, and nonalignment. In the speech, Arce explained that the FSLN had made these commitments simply to gain international support and thereby forestall possible U.S. intervention. For NSAs this is the real intent of the Sandinistas and the reason why pressure must be brought to bear on them to change.

In a February 21, 1985 news conference, President Reagan stated more clearly than before his belief that the goal of U.S. policy in Nicaragua must be to "change the character" of the Sandinista regime. The specific exchange is worth quoting.

Question: Mr. President, on Capitol Hill the other day [the] Secretary of State suggested that the goal of your policy now is to remove the Sandinista Government in Nicaragua. Is that your goal?

Answer: Well, remove it in the sense of its present structure, in which it is a Communist, totalitarian state and it is not a government chosen by its people. . . .

Question: To the question, aren't you advocating the overthrow of the present Government, if not to substitute another form of what you say was the revolution?

Answer: Not if the present Government would turn around and say—all right—if they'd say uncle, or all right, and come back over into the revolutionary Government and let's straighten this out and institute the goals.

Although there are legal and diplomatic reasons why a president of one country cannot publicly call for the overthrow of another legally recognized government, President Reagan came about as close as one can come to doing so. Perhaps the best way to sum up the President's statement is to say that, in his view, the Sandinista leopard must either change its spots or go.

It is not a meaningless question, then, whether U.S. support for anti-Sandinista rebels, military maneuvers in Honduras, economic reprisals, and other measures of the Reagan administration were designed to pressure the Sandinistas into making concessions, but still leave them in power, or to create conditions that would fuel internal dissent and, when combined with contra activities, lead to the overthrow of the Sandinista government.

A policy of pressure against the Sandinistas such as that recommended by NSAs has both positive and negative effects. NSAs emphasize the positive outcomes, HRAs the negative ones. For example, the U.S.-supported warfare on Nicaragua's borders with Honduras and Costa Rica has had both positive and negative results from the point of view of the stated objectives of U.S. policy. Nicaragua has taken steps typical of a country on a war footing: initiated a draft, militarized the society, limited dissent and the operation of a free press, and stigmatized the legitimate opposition as linked to the "treasonous" rebels. This reduction in domestic political freedom, even though it began before the contras received CIA support, can still be largely justified by the Sandinistas as being in response to the military pressure of the contra war. Economic dislocations caused in part by Sandinista mistakes as well as by economic sabotage can be blamed entirely on "Yankee aggression." HRAs emphasize that the most radical elements of the Sandinista leadership are strengthened politically against more moderate elements by the pressure from the United States. (Of course, these "negative" consequences are "positive" if the aim of U.S. policy is to make conditions so bad politically and economically that internal dissent is raised, leading to the overthrow of the regime and the installation of a new, and presumably better, replacement.)

The pressure also appears to have had "positive" results. Many NSAs and HRAs agree that the November 1984 elections were held by the Sandinistas in an attempt to relegitimize the government in Latin American and European eyes and to counteract U.S. hostility. La Prensa, the stridently anti-Sandinista newspaper which has become a symbol of press freedom to the outside world, would probably be shut down permanently by the Sandinistas if external pressure to preserve it did not exist.

Former Assistant Secretary of State Motley made the case for pressuring the Sandinistas succinctly and effectively in testimony to the Subcommittee on Western Hemisphere Affairs of the House Foreign Affairs Committee in early 1985:

- The Sandinistas have global ties and plans for Nicaragua and the rest of Central America that are contrary to U.S. interests;

- They will not modify or bargain over their position until there is some incentive for them to do so;

- The only incentive that has proved effective thus far has been opposition from other Nicaraguans. . . ;

- If pressure is taken away, the Sandinistas will have no reason to compromise;

- If the Sandinistas have no reason to compromise, Contadora will surely fail; and

- If Contadora fails, the long-run costs to the United States in terms of money and lives will be much greater. (*Current Policy* no. 655, p. 7.)

NSAs advocate such a policy of "coercive diplomacy"—ratcheting up the pressure on a diplomatic adversary to obtain agreement on certain clear objectives—against Nicaragua. Every president, they argue, has engaged in such tactics at one time or another. The stated objectives of the Reagan administration's "coercive diplomacy" toward Nicaragua were to force the Sandinistas to comply with their supposed commitment to the Organization of American States, to support democratic pluralism and respect human and civil rights, to reduce the size of Nicaragua's military force, to cut Nicaraguan military and security ties to Cuba and the Soviet bloc, and to end Nicaraguan support for guerrilla groups in neighboring countries.

HRAs are concerned, however, that if the Sandinistas are the confirmed Marxist-Leninists that NSAs say they are, they will never be willing to accept these conditions. At some point, additional pressure will no longer lead to further concessions on the Sandinistas' part but to the conviction that no response is acceptable but capitulation. At that point the Sandinistas may decide to harden their position.

HRAs point to the experience of late 1987 and 1988 as indicating that U.S. pressure to isolate and punish Nicaragua produced more negative than positive results. After signing the Esquipulas II peace agreement, Nicaragua restored full civil liberties, released a number of political prisoners, and established a National Reconciliation Commission headed by their most vocal critic, Cardinal Miguel Obando y Bravo. This was due, HRAs argue, not to the military and economic pressure of the United States, but to the moral authority exercised by President Arias of Costa Rica and the other Central American presidents who implicitly recognized the legitimacy of the Sandinista government. By early 1988 seven months of negotiations had produced more positive change in Nicaragua than had seven years of war. The cutoff of U.S. aid to the contras in February 1988 similarly led to the first direct talks between the Sandinistas and the contras.

NSAs emphasize the necessity for power and strength in any diplomatic encounter. They rely on U.S. military assets to play a large role in persuading opponents to accept agreements which they might otherwise resist. HRAs believe in the peaceful resolution of disputes as a principle. Agreements are only likely to endure, they argue, if they are the result of mutual concessions.

HRAs suspect the true objectives of the Reagan administration in Nicaragua were the overthrow of a radical experiment in social change that might both prosper and be less threatening to the United States if it were faced with less hostility. NSAs suspect the real goal of the Sandinistas to be a Marxist-Leninist state that would construct a communist "utopia" after the fashion of the Soviet Union and Cuba. Without the pressure of U.S. support for the contras, Nicaragua will become a source of irritation if not mortal danger to her neighbors and, through them, ultimately to the United States.

El Salvador

Question: Is the Conflict in El Salvador the Result of Political, Economic, and Social Problems or "a Textbook Case of Indirect Armed Aggression by Communist Powers through Cuba"?

Discussion:

Throughout the 1980s a debate raged in Washington over whether Central America should be defined as an East-West or a North-South problem. East-West problems are usually considered the cream of international issues, the ones that directly affect relations between the superpowers. Nuclear war, the security of Western Europe, the balance of strategic weapons—these are all examples of issues that influence the basic balance between the Soviet Union and the United States; a balance which has kept us at "cold war" for forty years, but has also prevented either of the superpowers from risking an attack on its rival. For NSAs, East-West issues are the "sexiest" of all policy issues because they concern the basic survival of the United States.

North-South issues deal instead with relations between the often newly independent states of the Third World (largely located south of the equator) and the wealthy, industrial, capitalist powers of the north. The North includes the older "imperial" powers of Europe whose former colonies now constitute the "Third World," and the United States, which had few colonial possessions but is viewed as the new "imperial" power of the post–Second World War era by many in the South. North-South issues generally concern economic questions such as trade, investment, and aid and usually involve demands by the South for assistance in their drive for improved standards of living. The issues also have political and social dimensions as much of the Third World is still struggling to create representative political institutions and to integrate regional, ethnic, or racial divisions into a national whole.

Defining the problems of Central America as North-South is to assert that the conflicts stem from the political, economic, and social problems common to the less-developed countries of the world. Central America is one of the poorest parts of Latin America, and there are great gaps between the poor majority and the wealthy few, who have ruled the region for decades. To argue that Central America is a North-South issue is to advocate that the challenges to the United States in the region stem from social, economic, and political causes indigenous to the region and that the U.S. response should primarily address these causes by supporting progressive social reform and promoting governments that are responsive to the needs of the majority.

To assert that Central America is an East-West issue is to focus on the Soviet Union (and its presumed instruments, Cuba and Nicaragua) as the source of problems in the region. President Reagan, for example, stated in a 1980 campaign interview that there would be no hot spots in the world were not the Soviet Union behind them. Expressed in this bald a fashion, the "East-West" optic sees all trouble for the United States in the world as stemming from Soviet (or other) communist machinations and not from indigenous developments or, for that matter, from problems that the United States had a hand in creating. Viewing an issue from an East-West perspective also defines it as a zero-sum game in which any advance by one side implies a loss by the other. To the extent that Central America is an East-West problem, the United States must become involved if for no other reason than to prevent a gain by the Soviet Union.

Few NSAs or HRAs view Central America as exclusively an East-West or a North-South problem, but there are important differences in emphasis between our two stereotypical policy types that have significant implications for future policy.

NSAs stress military aid as only one part of a much larger program of economic assistance and social reform in Central America designed to address the acknowledged North-South dimension of the problems. They insist, however, on the need for this military "shield" to protect the U.S. investment in economic and democratic development from communist attack and to allow this assistance to have effect. Marxist-Leninists, they argue, want to take advantage of local injustices and to use the population's anger to impose a new dictatorship that not only fails to address the injustices but imposes new tyrannies on an unwilling population. Communism, by definition, cannot be a freely chosen form of government for a nation; it is always imposed. Unless the military shield is there to protect a government under attack, no amount of reform will satisfy communist guerrillas bent on the installation of their dictatorship.

HRAs hold the United States responsible for neglecting, if not causing, many of Central America's problems. They note the appearance of effective leftist guerrillas in the region only after earlier attempts at reform had been thwarted by local elites solely concerned with the protection of their own privileged positions. They lament the short-sightedness of the United States in ignoring social problems and supporting groups opposed to any change. In the past, argue HRAs, in countries like Mexico and Guatemala, the United States' fear of communism led it to oppose true reformist movements that were mild compared to what the United States itself now tries to impose in countries such as El Salvador. Unless the United States remains focused primarily on the indigenous origins of the region's problems, it is likely to lose its way politically, choose the stability of a conservative regime over necessary change as it has done so often in the past, and encourage more radical and threatening developments in the future.

HRAs emphasize the historical amnesia that afflicts much of the policy-making community in Washington. They wonder, given the historical record, how long-term the commitment of some NSAs to reform would be if, magically, Soviet-Cuban sponsored insurgents were to disappear from Central America overnight. Given their emphasis on the external dimension of the Central American crisis, HRAs ask whether NSAs can be trusted to choose reform over stability in the day-to-day decisions required by the fluid and dynamic process occurring in El Salvador. Wouldn't the United States have deserted President Duarte, so far to the left ideologically from many NSAs, if the situation had stabilized sufficiently to permit a less reform-minded alternative?

HRAs charge that NSAs tend to forget past behavior that contributed to current dilemmas and to overreact to movements for social change. HRAs are in turn criticized by NSAs for seeming to ignore the changing realities of a better-armed and more active Cuba and of a Soviet Union more able than ever before to project its power far from its shores. Cuba did not create the problems in Central America nor, in most cases, the guerrilla forces that have arisen in the region. But, argue NSAs, it has played a crucial role at critical points in providing basic military training for many of the guerrilla leaders and in coordinating unified "fronts" of diverse guerrilla factions that proved more effective in waging war. It has never been easy to make true revolution anywhere in Latin America. However, the presence of Cuba is increasingly helping to change the balance of forces between those opposed to change, those supporting democratic reform, and those dedicated to the violent overthrow of the old system.

Some HRAs argue that emphasizing the North-South aspect of Central America's problems is, in fact, the best way for the United States to score points in the East-West game. They point out that the Soviet Union has very limited ability to offer what Third World countries need most—trade, aid, technology, and markets. Let radical regimes in Latin America rant and rave at the United States if they must. Eventually, if the United States shows forbearance, these regimes will come to recognize that the United States has too much to offer to be ignored or made the object of long-term hostility.

Whatever such an approach to radical change in Latin America might have to recommend it, NSAs argue that such a program could face some short-term political realities that would prohibit its being tried long enough to work. They point out that although the Soviet Union has limited economic and financial assistance to offer Third World countries, it does have something that can be of immediate and often decisive help: military aid. Directly or through Cuba or other allies, the Soviet Union can and has delivered the firepower (and, at times, the Cuban troops) that made the difference. The problems of governing, once power is achieved, may incline a new regime more toward the United States, but the earlier Soviet military aid at a moment of crisis gets the Soviets in on the ground floor of many new radical regimes.

The historical legacy of the United States in Latin America also weighs heavily in competition for the affections of radical regimes. For many in Latin America, not only the left, it is the United States, not the Soviet Union, that has historically constituted a threat to their countries. Because of its historic dominance of the region, the United States would probably be resented by its weaker and poorer Latin American neighbors even if its past behavior had been a model of relations between big and small powers. The United States was not, of course, such a model.

The United States can expect, then, to be viewed skeptically, if not with outright hostility, by left-of-center governments in Latin America. It may have to endure years of venomous rhetoric and actions designed to show a new radical regime's independence of and contempt for "Yankee imperialism." Relations with Cuba and the Soviet Union, if not already strong because of past military help and ideological affinities, will be developed to act as a counterweight to the power of the United States in the hemisphere. Indeed, these ties will be sought precisely because they are the one sore point through which the new government can have some impact on Washington.

The policy recommendation of HRAs that the United States be

the "faithful suitor" of leftist regimes in Latin America calls for a great deal of patience on the part of U.S. leaders and the general public. The political difficulties of maintaining a policy that only seems rewarded by anti-U.S. rhetoric and actions over a single administration, let alone between administrations of different parties, are formidable.

NSAs point out that such a policy toward the revolution in Nicaragua was, in fact, tried and ran into these difficulties. After great ambivalence on the part of the Carter administration toward the ouster of Somoza, the United States offered a generous aid package to the Sandinistas and exercised forbearance in the hope that the hostile rhetoric would eventually diminish and not lead to actions inimical to U.S. interests. Aid was finally suspended when it became clear to the Carter administration that the Sandinistas were significantly aiding the Salvadoran guerrillas. Carter's ambassador to Nicaragua, Lawrence Pezzullo, argues that his strong criticism of the arms flow to the guerrillas resulted in a cutback and that such a carrot-and-stick policy toward the Sandinistas would have worked to moderate the regime over time. He was never proven right or wrong because the Reagan administration cancelled the aid package in April 1981 and pursued a stick-and-stick policy toward Nicaragua thereafter. NSAs question whether even the Carter administration could have sustained the carrot-and-stick approach over the years, not just months, that might have been required to moderate and contain the Sandinista revolution. Would political support in the Congress and among the public have been there even if Carter had been reelected?

Question: Should the United States Assist the Salvadoran Government to Win the War against the Leftist Guerrillas Militarily or Urge the Government to Seek Some Form of Negotiated Settlement?

Discussion:

The war in El Salvador has been going on since 1979. Perhaps as many as 70,000 lives have been lost, the majority of them civilians rather than soldiers or guerrillas. As a result of the violence, nearly 10 percent of El Salvador's population of five million has been driven into internal or external exile. It would seem evident that an end to the conflict would be most people's top priority, and it is. But opinions differ widely about how to achieve real and enduring peace in El Salvador.

One option not seriously considered by either NSAs or HRAs in the 1980s that may return to the options list in the 1990s is that chosen by the United States in Vietnam: withdrawal. By the end of the Reagan administration many observers could almost feel a weariness on the part of Washington for dealing with Central America. The inconclusive results of the massive U.S. support and the increasing concern about budget deficits threatened to produce a reaction against continued U.S. involvement.

Most analysts believe that withdrawal of support by the United States would result in a victory by the left. Some HRAs, persuaded of the good intentions of the guerrillas and of their civilian political allies, see the establishment of a leftist government dedicated to reform and social justice as producing stability in El Salvador. NSAs, who view the guerrillas and their supporters as Marxist-Leninists, see a leftist victory as the first in a series of destabilizing losses that could enflame the entire region. El Salvador itself might be pacified under a totalitarian system, but its revolutionary government would try to extend its radical politics beyond its borders in cooperation or perhaps even in competition with neighboring Nicaragua. Agreeing with the domino theory, NSAs argue that victory for the left in El Salvador would be the beginning, not the end, of conflict in the region and of security threats to the United States.

A second option advocated by some NSAs but not an officially declared goal of the United States is military victory by the Salvadoran government. In this option, diplomatic negotiations can be part of an overall strategy for defeating the guerrillas, but cannot replace military victory as the ultimate goal of U.S. policy. Otherwise, anti-U.S. guerrilla forces in other parts of the world will feel free to wage armed subversion in pursuit of military victory without risking ultimate defeat or destruction. Should their circumstances become desperate, they can try to negotiate a settlement with the United States that leaves them in a position to subvert from within or to return to a guerrilla strategy when conditions permit a change in tactics.

HRAs counter that the price of military victory will be high, if it can be achieved. Official estimates are that there are roughly 4,000 to 6,500 guerrillas. To achieve a military victory, most of the actual fighters would need to be killed, captured, or forced to surrender or to leave the country. In addition, it is estimated that for every guerrilla fighter there are roughly three to ten *masas*, or civilian supporters, of the guerrillas. Some of the 12,000 to 65,000 *masas* would undoubtedly desert a losing guerrilla cause. But other passive or active supporters of the guerrillas, now branded as "subversives," would face the same fate as the guerrillas.

To achieve military victory, the Salvadoran armed forces will need to be increased beyond their present size of a little over 54,000 men. A ratio used in classic discussions of guerrilla warfare is that to defeat a guerrilla army, a conventional army must outnumber it by ten to one. If this ratio were to hold in El Salvador, the Salvadoran army might need to more than double its present size. This would entail the obvious economic expenditures by El Salvador (and, indirectly, by the United States) for training, salaries, and equipment. U.S. economic and military assistance well beyond the $3 billion provided since 1980 would be required. In addition, there are the difficult-to-calculate political costs to El Salvador's fledgling democratic institutions of its armed forces growing to nearly twice their present size, given a history of military intervention in politics. At least one of El Salvador's neighbors, Honduras, already feels threatened by the size of the well-equipped Salvadoran army, having fought a "Soccer War" with El Salvador in 1969.

An all-out effort to defeat the guerrillas militarily will also exact a price in civilian casualties. The kind of counterinsurgency warfare involving "model villages," "free-fire" zones and the use of aerial bombing that the Salvadoran armed forces must employ to try to win the war has traditionally had a high cost in civilian casualties.

There are too many variables to make a reliable calculation of the human costs of an attempt to win a military victory in El Salvador. Some NSAs believe that a victory drive by the Salvadoran armed forces with the full backing and funding of the United States would lead to a precipitous collapse of the guerrilla forces. HRAs believe that such massive violence by the government would radicalize the civilian population and lead to greater support for the guerrillas. All agree that tens of thousands of lives would be lost in the struggle.

NSAs, convinced that the Soviet Union is orchestrating a strategy for eventual domination of the hemisphere, see these costs as acceptable if, as a result of their military defeat in El Salvador, the communists are dissuaded from attempting armed subversion elsewhere. In this grey area between ideological competition and all-out war, where communist forces are seen as having an advantage, the United States would have demonstrated, as it did not in Vietnam, that it can defeat guerrilla forces at their own game. For those who view El Salvador in these terms, almost any cost would be worthwhile in order to deliver such a setback to the communists' global strategy.

For HRAs the pursuit of military victory in El Salvador would be a disaster on a scale unprecedented since Vietnam. Aside from the costs to El Salvador in lives lost on all sides, the drive toward military victory could reopen wounds in the U.S. body politic that are just now beginning to heal. Escalating warfare costing tens of thousands of lives that was a direct outcome of U.S. policy could well, in the view of HRAs, reignite the protests and internal divisions of the Vietnam era even if carried out by the Salvadorans themselves. If, however, the Salvadoran army faltered and the United States assumed a direct combat role—a possibility if not a probability—severe domestic repercussions would result. Valuable strategic resources from other parts of the world would be diverted to the traditionally low-priority area of the Caribbean Basin and anti-U.S. sentiment in Latin America boosted at a time when the emergence of new democracies there had given hope for better hemispheric relations. Before it had time to develop a new consensus about its role in the Third World in the post-Iran and post-Afghanistan era, the United States would be plunged into another conflict whose casualties and refugees would make themselves felt directly at home.

A third possible path to peace in El Salvador is a negotiated solution that somehow reconciles the guerrillas and their supporters with the government and the army. There are few if any precedents for resolving a deeply divisive conflict like El Salvador's by negotiation. But faced with the costs of the alternatives—withdrawal or military victory—many HRAs look to a negotiated solution with hope.

How would a negotiated end to the war work? When President Duarte called for a dialogue with the guerrillas in 1984, there were undoubtedly some who hoped that a five-year war that had cost

IS EL SALVADOR SPANISH FOR VIETNAM?

Adviser—Vietnam-era term for Trainer (see **Trainer**).
Trainer—Central America–era term for Adviser.
    —"Salvospeak," *Soldier of Fortune* magazine (March 1985).

As U.S. involvement in El Salvador has increased, many HRAs have tried to draw analogies between El Salvador and Vietnam. The object of the analogies, of course, is to alarm public opinion by suggesting that the United States is taking the same course pursued in Vietnam with such disastrous results: more than 50,000 dead, the first U.S. military defeat in modern times, the "loss" of Vietnam, Laos, and Cambodia to communism, and fractures in our domestic social fabric that continue to the present.

As in other debates over Central America, those who argue for and against comparing El Salvador to Vietnam are usually talking past each other. When they raise the specter of Vietnam, most HRAs are suggesting that the United States is entering another conflict, without understanding its fundamental nature, that has the potential to divide American public opinion and undermine confidence in the nation's institutions. For HRAs, Vietnam was a local conflict in which the United States should not have become involved or should have tried to solve by diplomatic rather than military means. "Victory" in Vietnam was not possible at costs commensurate with the interests at stake for the United States.

For NSAs, Vietnam represents a defeat that the United States need not and should not have suffered. A noble effort, U.S. involvement in Vietnam was undermined by radical opposition in the United States and political leaders who restrained the military from devoting the resources necessary to win the battle. For NSAs, the war in Vietnam was lost in the streets, the U.S. media, and the White House, not on the battlefield. It should and could have been won.

When a reporter asked President Reagan in a March 1981 press conference if El Salvador could become another Vietnam and he replied that it could not because El Salvador is much closer to the United States and because the United States is not just aiding El Salvador but defending the entire Western Hemisphere from a takeover by communism, HRAs saw his response as a *non sequitur* or as a confirmation of their worst fears.

Former Assistant Secretary for Inter-American Affairs Motley has discussed the Vietnam analogy in a useful way. In testimony before the

Subcommittee on Western Hemisphere Affairs of the House Foreign Affairs Committee in 1985, he said:

> There are two things that the vast majority of the American people do not want in this region so close to home: they do not want a second Cuba, and they do not want a second Vietnam. By a second Cuba, I mean the institutionalization of another well-armed communist state, this time on the mainland, supported by the Soviet Union and working actively against U.S. interests and friends in the region.
>
> And, by a second Vietnam, I mean a prolonged conflict involving U.S. combat troops with no clear goal and no end in sight consistent with the protection of strategic American interests.
>
> It is true that some Americans are concerned with one and not the other: some would risk another Vietnam to prevent another Cuba, while others are so concerned with any sign of a second Vietnam that they ignore the threat of a second Cuba. But the majority of our fellow citizens seek and will support a policy which serves our interests while preventing both a new Cuba and a new Vietnam.

Secretary Motley is probably correct in arguing that the prevention of a new Cuba or a new Vietnam sets the limits for the broadest consensus on Central American policy. NSAs believe they are pursuing such a course by increasing assistance to the Salvadoran government and to the Nicaraguan rebels while limiting direct U.S. military involvement. If this strategy is as successful as NSAs believe it will be, another Cuba and another Vietnam would be prevented.

HRAs point out, however, that in their efforts to gain support for this policy, NSAs have defined the importance of Central America to the United States in increasingly dramatic terms. It is now seen as a vital interest of the United States and significant U.S. prestige has been attached to our ability to influence the outcome of events in the region. If the current policy of massive assistance and limited direct U.S. military support fails to defeat the Salvadoran guerrillas and unseat the Sandinistas, the United States will be faced with the option of accepting a blow to its prestige or escalating the level of direct U.S. commitment. This is precisely what happened in Vietnam. Each time the choice was faced the option of escalation was elected until the disintegration of support for the war at home forced withdrawal and even greater defeat for U.S. interests and prestige.

Thus, for HRAs, the verdict is still out on whether El Salvador is, as the bumper stickers say, Spanish for Vietnam.

tens of thousands of lives could be settled merely by meetings and talks. More realistically, the recognition of each side implied by the face-to-face meeting was but the first step in a very long process of reconciliation that has the odds stacked against it.

The initial meetings between the guerrillas (the FMLN) and their political representatives (the FDR) and the Salvadoran government produced two sets of positions that have led to a stalemate. President Duarte argued on behalf of the government that the conditions of civil strife, repression, death squads, and military-dominated politics that had produced and perhaps justified the escalation of armed conflict in 1979 were now on their way to being removed. The process of reform and democratization represented by President Duarte was sufficiently under way for the FDR-FMLN to renounce armed struggle, accept the new constitution of 1984 drawn up by a Legislative Assembly dominated by the right wing, and rejoin the political process as citizen participants. Essentially, this was a position that called on the guerrillas to admit that their costly fight was no longer justified and to accept that forces in the army and the death squads, which had fought viciously against them, were to become the guardians of their safe reintegration into civil society.

The guerrillas for their part demanded to be considered as a virtual government-in-exile. They refused to accept the rules of the political game set out in a 1984 constitution which they had had no part in developing. They called, therefore, for the delegitimization of the electoral process that had brought Duarte to power and the development of a new constitution, new elections, and a new army that would integrate the guerrilla fighters into the traditional armed forces. Subsequent meetings between the government and the guerrillas in 1987 under the auspices of Esquipulas II have not significantly altered these initial stands.

The positions of the government and the guerrillas are, as currently stated, irreconcilable. NSAs believe that the guerrillas, as Marxists, will never negotiate in good faith for a democratic solution and are not surprised that the guerrillas would propose unacceptable conditions. They urge the Salvadoran government to continue the talks for the sake of appearances while prosecuting the war to the fullest. HRAs argue that these initial statements may only represent the opening of a bargaining process that will become more serious over time. Few expected that such negotiations would ever have occurred in the first place, but they did, due largely to President Duarte's forceful personality and vision of himself as the savior of his country. It is not inconceivable, HRAs argue, that future breakthroughs could occur.

HRAs believe that the future of the negotiations will be strongly affected by two central actors in El Salvador—the U.S. government and the Salvadoran military. Although supportive (after the fact) of Duarte's overtures to the guerrillas made in his speech to the United Nations in October 1984, the United States seemed to many HRAs to be genuinely surprised by his bold step. HRAs are also made uneasy by the commitment of many NSAs to a military victory over the guerrillas that would "send a message" to other insurgency movements in the region and throughout the world. HRAs point out that most NSAs remain opposed to any type of "power-sharing" arrangement in which the guerrillas gain some form of participation in the government outside the framework of the present constitution.

NSAs insist that the guerrillas participate in elections, and they repeatedly state their aversion to the guerrillas "shooting their way into power." NSAs believe that "power sharing" would reward the guerrillas for their violent actions, encourage other groups to employ similar tactics, and, ultimately, be used by the guerrillas to subvert a democratic government from within.

A second key group limiting the possibility of negotiations is the Salvadoran military. There is a raging debate over the true nature of the Salvadoran military: are they reform-minded patriots or silent partners of the death squads? Both elements continue to coexist in the military and each has gained dominance at one point or another in Salvadoran history.

Former Minister of Defense General Vides Casanova, who accompanied President Duarte to the first peace talks in La Palma, and much of the high command were viewed as supporters of President Duarte, based on Duarte's ability to command respect abroad and to obtain the U.S. Congressional funding essential to meet the country's economic and military needs. In the 1985 legislative elections from which Duarte's party emerged the surprising victor, the armed forces solidly opposed attempts by the losing right-wing parties to discredit the results of the elections. For his part, Duarte went to great lengths to praise the military, exhort it to greater efforts against the guerrillas, and to act as an effective commander in chief whom the armed forces could respect.

However, even before the defeat of the Christian Democrats in the legislative elections of 1988 and the diagnosis of President Duarte's terminal cancer, the military had grown increasingly disillusioned with El Salvador's political leaders. In the military's view, the war against the guerrillas is 90 percent political and 10 percent military. By this they mean that the principal weapon to defeat the guerrillas is a stable and prosperous government, able to distribute goods and services to the population and, thereby, increase their loyalty to the government. The corruption and inefficiency of the Christian Democrats became, in the minds of the military, the most important obstacle to their final victory over the guerrillas.

A critical point will come if talks ever move beyond the irreconcilable stage at which they currently stand. Issues such as "power sharing" and a role for the guerrilla fighters in the nation's armed forces have the potential to cause deep divisions within the military. At this point, HRAs believe, the role of the United States will become crucial. The United States will have several tools at its disposal, such as linking future aid to the Salvadoran government and military to progress in the negotiations, that could support the negotiation process. Or it could frustrate negotiations by encouraging those politicians and military officers opposed to any agreement with the guerrillas. If such a moment arrives, the debate between NSAs and HRAs over whether to pursue military victory with its toll in human lives, or the difficult and dangerous road of negotiations will decide the future of U.S. relations with El Salvador.

At this point, you are probably somewhat pessimistic about the future of El Salvador. The options of withdrawal and military victory have high costs. Negotiations to produce a political settlement appear less costly in human terms, but seem exceedingly difficult. There are no easy solutions. The "options list" of the NSA and the HRA are relatively short and very problematic. Meanwhile, the war drags on.

Honduras

Question: Does the U.S. Military Buildup in Honduras Serve U.S. Interests?

Discussion:

Beginning in early 1984, the United States engaged in a large buildup of U.S. forces either temporarily or permanently staged in Honduras. Since 1983 there have been eight major joint U.S.-Honduran military maneuvers, each involving between 1,000 and 25,000 U.S. troops. "Temporary" installations have also been built and a regional military training center established to instruct Salvadoran and Honduran armed forces.

NSAs deny that the buildup in Honduras is out of the ordinary, but admit that the maneuvers and other activities are part of a campaign of pressure against Nicaragua. HRAs charge that the buildup has converted Honduras into a virtual land-bound aircraft carrier poised on Nicaragua's border to intimidate and, ultimately, assist in the toppling of the Sandinista regime.

If one assumes with NSAs that the Sandinistas are determined to become another Cuba and can be deterred from this course only by persuasion of force, the buildup in Honduras makes a great deal of sense. Former Under Secretary of Defense for Policy Fred C. Iklé stated in September 1983 that the consolidation of the Sandinista regime in Nicaragua would necessitate the "partition" of Central America and that the United States would have to "man a new military front line of the East-West conflict, right here on our continent." By this he meant that a hostile Nicaragua, aligned with the Soviet Union, would require the permanent stationing of U.S. troops, as in South Korea and West Germany, in countries bordering Nicaragua to prevent the Sandinistas from sweeping throughout the isthmus. If the Sandinistas have such intentions and U.S. policy does not deter them from this goal or lack of Congressional support undermines U.S. policy, the military buildup in Honduras will be seen as prescient. Meanwhile, argue NSAs, the massive presence of U.S. forces keeps pressure on the Sandinistas, discourages Nicaragua from crossing into Honduras to wipe out the headquarters of the FDN, the largest branch of the contras, and ties down substantial numbers of Nicaraguan forces that might otherwise be used to attack the guerrillas on Nicaragua's southern border or in overseas adventures such as those of Cuba.

HRAs are in general less persuaded than NSAs of Nicaragua's aggressive intentions, but also are convinced that the buildup and a policy of military pressure may hasten rather than discourage hostile behavior by the Sandinistas. (See "Nicaragua" section in this chapter.)

They are worried about the impact of the buildup in several other areas. One is the way in which the buildup reinforces stereotypes about the United States as an "imperial" power and recalls the era of "gunboat diplomacy" when the United States dictated terms to many Central American countries. They also believe that the strong military stance adopted by the United States undermines rather than supports the Esquipulas II accords which seek negotiated solutions to the region's conflicts.

While the heavy U.S. presence undoubtedly serves as a tripwire to warn the Sandinistas that incursions into Honduras will produce a response by the United States, HRAs worry that it also exposes the United States to being inadvertently drawn into hostilities. Reconnaissance flights, routine helicopter trips near the border, the support of private U.S. citizens for the contras, and the ferrying of Honduran troops to border areas to repel Sandinista incursions all have the potential to produce confrontations that could escalate out of control.

Great debate exists as well over the impact of the buildup on U.S.-Honduran relations. NSAs argue that the only thing that could damage U.S.-Honduran relations is if the United States failed to support Honduras strongly enough. In this view, the Hondurans are in favor of progressively closer ties with the United States to protect them from a better-armed and ideologically incompatible Nicaragua. If the United States maintains itself as a firm and resolute ally, no problems will arise between the two countries.

HRAs counter that this perspective on Honduras was given a jolt in 1984 when the head of the Honduran armed forces, General Gustavo Alvarez Martínez, was ousted by his fellow military officers. A *lider máximo* (maximum leader) in the classic Latin American style, Alvarez had alienated his fellow officers by his arrogant disregard for collegial decision making within the armed forces and for being identified too closely with U.S. interests. His replacement, General Walter López, while still friendly to the United States, made it clear that friendship had a higher price than the one exacted by General Alvarez. On the issues of tacit Honduran support for the contras, the training of Salvadorans in the regional military training center in Honduras, and the renegotiation of security and economic relations between the United States and Honduras, General López was a much tougher bargainer. General Regalado, the current commander in chief, has continued to demand improved terms from the U.S.-Honduran security relationship. HRAs point to these developments as early warning signs that the increased U.S. presence in Honduras, while convenient in the short run, would set off forces in the longer term that will ultimately weaken Honduras and the good relations that Honduras and the United States currently enjoy. The anti-U.S. demonstrations in 1988 only confirmed these fears.

A final concern of HRAs about the U.S. buildup in Honduras is that U.S. military aid was diverted to the contras in violation of Congressional prohibitions. Press reports to this effect have been denied by the Reagan administration. While asserting that congressional funds were used for the purposes for which they were approved, Secretary of State Shultz did affirm the right of sovereign countries who are allies of the United States to use their own funds in any way they see fit. For HRAs this is yet another example of executive branch subversion of congressional law. For NSAs it underscores the dilemma posed by the intrusion of Congress into the foreign policy–making prerogatives of the executive branch.

Question: Does the U.S. Buildup in Honduras Serve Honduran Interests?

Discussion:

Some NSAs would consider this question an example of the arrogance of U.S. attitudes toward Latin America that is at the heart of U.S.–Latin American problems. If the Honduran people through their elected government desire closer ties with the United States and encourage a large U.S. presence in their country, why should the United States preoccupy itself with whether this is really in the interest of Honduras?

The answer for HRAs goes to the admitted fragility of Honduran democracy and the effects on its new democratic practices of a heavy U.S. presence. As we saw in the Honduran "snapshot" in chapter 2, Honduras has only recently broken a tradition of rule by military strongmen with the election of civilian governments in 1981 and 1985. While an encouraging sign, these recent steps are far from making Honduras into a bastion of democracy.

With a largely uneducated and unintegrated rural population, Honduran democracy is so far largely a game for urban elites. The military remains a powerful force behind the throne and has made several public displays of its independence from civilian rule, the most egregious example being General López's announcement of the renegotiation of a U.S.-Honduran security treaty in 1983 without apparent consultation with President Suázo Córdoba.

When asked if Hondurans were not pleased by the massive U.S. presence, a Honduran lawyer and social commentator once remarked to an HRA: "Absolutely—especially the prostitutes." What he was implying is that despite payoffs to Honduras, the U.S. buildup has certain inevitable and probably unavoidable corrupting influences on Honduran life.

One is the elevation of the U.S. ambassador to the "proconsul" role that characterized all-powerful U.S. ambassadors in the region fifty years ago. In the first decades of the twentieth century, the U.S. ambassador in Caribbean and Central American countries was the second most powerful person in the country—or at times the most powerful. Presidents and dictators consulted the U.S. ambassador about the details of domestic political life, and military generals tested the reactions of their colleagues at the U.S. embassy before mounting any coups.

The buildup in Honduras and the organizing of the contra activities based in Honduras have now placed the U.S. ambassador in this "proconsul" role again. Anti-American sentiment in Honduras is growing. The prominent position of the U.S. ambassador lends credence to those opposed to the current government who charge that Honduran independence and autonomy are being trampled by the heavy U.S. presence.

Another consequence for Honduras of the buildup is the increased importance given to the military. The Honduran military is now the power behind the throne of a fragile Honduran democracy. While supportive of civilian rule thus far, the military retains a veto over future political developments. The intended impact of the U.S.

buildup on Honduran forces is, NSAs argue, to expand, upgrade, and professionalize them. Professionalization means in U.S. terms that they would become an effective but apolitical force concerned with the country's national security and uninvolved in politics.

While this may be the intention of U.S. policy, the historical record of similar efforts causes HRAs to be concerned about the ultimate impact on the Honduran political system of a more confident, better trained and armed, and larger military force. In El Salvador, the closest and most recent example, U.S. aid to the military seemed to have helped control some of its repressive instincts, but abuses by the army are again on the rise.

In the 1960s and 1970s U.S. training of Latin American military forces had no discernible effect on reinforcing civilian rule and democratic practices. Indeed, some HRAs argue that the military governments that came to power in Brazil, Argentina, Chile, Uruguay, and other countries were encouraged to think they could do better than civilian politicians as a result of the training and professionalization they had received from the United States and from their own military schools.

HRAs think that any analyst of Latin American affairs would have to be concerned about a policy in Honduras that emphasizes the military dimension as much as the Reagan administration did. Many Hondurans complain that, despite massive U.S. economic and military aid ($250 million in 1987), the military is consuming larger and larger portions of the meager budget available to the government of a poor country such as Honduras. The U.S. buildup is, according to HRAs, at least distorting Honduras's spending priorities and perhaps subtly undermining its infant democratic system.

HRAs feel that anyone familiar with U.S.–Latin American relations would have to wonder, finally, about the long-run impact on Honduras of the massive U.S. presence. In some ways, Honduras was one of the sleepier Central American countries, less polarized by the divisive forces that threatened to tear apart neighbors such as El Salvador and Guatemala and that produced revolution in Nicaragua. HRAs believe that the U.S. presence could accelerate a radicalization of Honduran politics rather than reinforce democracy.

HRAs observe that many of the countries that have had political

upheavals threatening to the United States were those which earlier in the twentieth century had experienced intense relations
with, and at times occupations by, the United States (Cuba, the
Dominican Republic, Nicaragua, Mexico). NSAs counter that it
would be incorrect to draw any direct causal links between the
earlier experience of U.S. dominance and later turmoil or to argue
that every incidence of heavy involvement by the United States
leads to revolutions aimed against the United States.

However, HRAs argue that it is easy for an overwhelming presence by the United States in a Latin American country to create a
convenient scapegoat for the opposition and perhaps help to radicalize that opposition. Those supported by the United States, because of the compromises they must inevitably make to gain U.S.
favor, are often portrayed by their opposition as *vendepatrias,* sell-
outs, who surrender national interests for the rewards that a great
power can bestow. Opposition figures, who under other circumstances might have to promote their cause on the merits of alternative policies, can take the easier demagogic road of condemning
U.S. imperialism as the source of all their country's problems.

Many Americans, raised on images of U.S. troops being received
as liberators by grateful Europeans in two world wars, have a hard
time understanding the intense hostility displayed toward the
United States in many Third World countries. The explanation for
this hostility, according to HRAs, is that in the Third World the
United States often intervenes not to save a whole people from a
foreign invader but to support one political faction against another.
Factions seeking U.S. help have learned to present their case as a
struggle to protect their nation against the threat of Communism.
This kind of intervention is welcomed by some but condemned by
others who are defeated because of U.S. support for their adversaries.

Thus, HRAs argue, U.S. policy makers need to be concerned
about the long-term effects of the U.S. buildup on Honduras's
domestic political process and on relations with the United States.
Many Hondurans, including the prostitutes, may be pleased with
the heavy U.S. presence. But the buildup has certain inevitable
side effects that may not be in the best long-term interests of either
the United States or Honduras. As is the case with the next country
to be discussed, Costa Rica, HRAs worry that U.S. policy in Hon-

duras runs the risk of sacrificing the long-term stability of Honduras to short-run strategic gains represented by the military buildup.

If pressed, NSAs might have to concede some truth, at least in the abstract, to each of these concerns of HRAs. But they would argue that, while different policies would be desirable in a more perfect world, the United States has to deal with the harsh reality of an increasingly well-armed and hostile Nicaragua sitting on Honduras's border. In the view of NSAs, the only way to deter the Sandinistas from aggression against their neighbors is to maintain the pressure on them that the contras have provided. To support the contras, to reassure Honduras and the other Central American countries that the United States will not abandon them to the Marxists, and to be prepared to contain Nicaragua if current policies do not succeed, the United States must play a large role in Honduras. If the consequences of a diminished U.S. presence in Honduras and the rest of Central America are that the Sandinistas are allowed to consolidate themselves in power and to act with a free hand in the region, that would be worse than anything happening now.

Costa Rica

Question: What Is the Best Way for Costa Rica to Protect Itself from a Potentially Hostile Nicaragua and Preserve Its Unique Democratic System: Neutrality, or Alliance with the United States?

Discussion:

Costa Rica is different from the rest of Central America in many ways. Literate, healthy, moderate in life-style as well as politics, Costa Rica is a breath of cool air to the visitor suffocating from travels to the "hot spots" of Central America. Yet Costa Rica in the late 1980s is feeling the pressures and the polarization of the conflicts raging all around it. Its population is becoming increasingly concerned about the course of the Sandinista revolution in bordering Nicaragua and divided over the best response to it.

As we saw in chapter 2, Costa Rica has been historically isolated from many events shaping the rest of Central America. Undoubtedly, that is a tradition that many Costa Ricans would like to continue. The government of President Luis Albert Monge (1982–

86), responding to this sentiment, proclaimed Costa Rica's "perpetual, active and unarmed neutrality" on November 17, 1983. Staying neutral while the rest of Central America flies apart at the seams has not been easy for Monge's successor, Oscar Arias. Costa Rican opposition groups, the country's free but conservative press, and some insistent NSA voices in the United States, argue that neutrality is an exercise in self-deception when a struggle between democracy and communism is being waged on their doorstep. They fear that with only a poorly equipped Rural and Civil Guard, Costa Rica will not be able to defend itself from an aggressive Sandinista state that desires to "export revolution" in order to maintain its own security. Even if Nicaragua does not threaten Costa Rica directly, they say, it may take advantage of the country's severe economic crisis to sow subversion. Costa Rican conservatives view the Sandinistas as Marxist-Leninists who can never be trusted to abide by agreements. They oppose all talks, negotiations, or agreements between Nicaragua and the United States, and are convinced that only the unseating of the Sandinistas will restore peace in the region. They want to align Costa Rica with a U.S. policy of pressure on the Sandinistas and to increase Costa Rica's military preparedness to resist them.

Those favoring the policy of neutrality also expect to have problems with Nicaragua in the future. But they contend that too close an alliance with the United States can only encourage the Sandinistas to take reprisals against Costa Rica as hostility mounts between the United States and Nicaragua. Training a few more guardsmen will not equip Costa Rica to do battle with the vastly superior Nicaraguan armed forces. It will, however, signal Costa Rica's alignment with a policy of confrontation. For many in Costa Rica, Honduras is a telling example of a country that has prostituted itself to U.S. interests, surrendering substantial sovereignty while receiving few benefits.

HRAs point out that Costa Ricans in general have a very benevolent view of the United States. They never suffered occupation or invasion by the "colossus of the North." There is little appreciation among the general public of the potential divergence between Costa Rica's interests as a tiny outpost of democracy and the global concerns of the superpower. Most would find it hard to believe that the United States would use up a country and throw it away when the costs became too high and political support withered at home, although this is what happened to another neutral country surrounded by conflict, Cambodia.

Question: How Can the United States Best Reinforce Costa Rica's Democratic Traditions?

Discussion:

As Costa Ricans debate among themselves the best direction for their country, NSAs urge the United States to press Costa Rica for a closer alliance. From the NSAs' perspective, Costa Rica needs to get its house in order if it is to resist the aggression being waged by communist forces throughout the region. Part of getting its house in order will be to give its economic policies a more free-market orientation and to join with the other U.S. allies, El Salvador and Honduras, in presenting a united front to the Marxist-Leninists in Nicaragua.

There is no question that Costa Rica's democratic traditions are threatened by its desperate economic condition. The revolution of 1948 that began the country's democratic tradition also created one of the first "welfare states" in the Western Hemisphere. While coffee prices were good and the economy prospered, Costa Rica could afford to provide reasonably well for its citizens, giving many, especially the middle class, a stake in the democratic system. The economic reversals of the 1970s that affected most of the Third World struck Costa Rica particularly hard. But instead of cutting back on its welfare policies, Costa Rica borrowed heavily, hoping for a future upturn in the economy that never came. Costa Rica in the mid-1980s is in desperate financial straits and has the dubious distinction of having the highest per-capita debt in Latin America.

Since 1983, the United States has been providing high levels of economic aid to Costa Rica—over $325 million in 1986 and 1987. As is standard practice, the United States (and international financial institutions) have urged, and in some cases required, changes in Costa Rican economic policies that they view as necessary to assure better performance in the future. These recommendations call for a reduction of the government's role in the economy and an increased emphasis on private-sector initiatives. One particularly sensitive issue has been a call by the United States for a denationalization of Costa Rica's banking system. As a key aspect of the

1948 program of reform, maintaining the banking system in public hands has been of great political importance to the Costa Ricans, and is one recommendation they have so far ignored.

The Costa Ricans find themselves in the very difficult position that was faced by another small welfare state in Latin America, Uruguay. Like Costa Rica, Uruguay experienced a middle-class revolution that created an advanced social welfare state, but early in the twentieth century. Financed by grain and beef production, Uruguay's social programs were the basis of a consensual democratic system that lasted until the 1970s. The progressive erosion of Uruguay's economy, however, undermined stability and promoted urban guerrilla warfare that, in turn, produced the classic repressive military reaction. Uruguay returned to democratic practice in 1985 after twelve years of a brutal military dictatorship.

Like Uruguay, Costa Rica can no longer afford the welfare state that has underwritten democratic politics for the last four decades. It must discover new sources of wealth or reach a new consensus about how to distribute wealth within the society. Neither of these alternatives will be easy in the midst of a regional war, domestic polarization, and economic crisis.

NSAs urge the United States to help this process by providing economic assistance to ease the transition. The United States should make clear to Costa Rica that the aid is to support a period of reexamination and the making of hard choices, not a way to avoid decisions that may have high political costs.

HRAs fear that in the midst of what the United States perceives as a grave threat to its security from Communism, NSAs will place more emphasis on gaining Costa Rica's support for its regional objectives than on encouraging dialogue among Costa Ricans as to the best course for their country, economically and politically. The United States, HRAs argue, will have to resist the temptation to equate the interests of a small, fragile democracy with its own interests as a superpower in preserving U.S. prerogatives in the region. This will be a tremendous challenge for the United States— one that it has not often met before in its relations with small powers.

Guatemala

Question: Does Guatemala's Ruthless and Apparently Successful Elimination of Its Guerrilla Threat Provide Lessons for Other Central American Countries?

Discussion:

Due to the unwillingness of its military government to comply with President Carter's human rights requirements, Guatemala did not receive U.S. assistance for or oversight of its armed forces in the late 1970s. Training and equipment were available from other countries without restrictions, but on a reduced basis. By all accounts, the lack of aid and supervision created a do-or-die situation that forced the Guatemalan armed forces back on their own resources. Without the mobility provided by imported helicopters, the army relied on decentralized command structures and extensive patrolling of guerrilla-held territory that put the armed forces into direct contact with the local population. The armed forces resolved to dry up the "sea" of largely Indian peasants in which the guerrillas swam (the classic analogy between guerrillas and peasants and fish in the sea comes from one of the most successful practitioners of guerrilla warfare, Mao Zedong) and adopted a series of measures to accomplish this. These included "civic action" programs that provided work and food for peasants in return for their recruitment into civil self-defense patrols (the so-called *frijoles y fusiles* or "beans and bullets" program). Nominally, every peasant male between the ages of 18 and 60 was required to join his local patrol. The patrols were to monitor suspicious activities in their villages, patrol local roads and paths, and participate in army-led sweeps of the area and in training exercises. "Model villages" were created into which thousands of peasants were moved so that they could be watched by the army and prevented from becoming a support base for the guerrillas.

Between 1980 and 1982, the army waged a brutal war in the countryside, killing thousands of peasants and community leaders who were suspected (or merely accused) of sympathizing with the guerrillas. The coup of March 1982, which brought General Efraín Ríos Montt to power, resulted in a decline in political murders and kidnappings in urban areas. The civil-defense strategy already described was adopted and the rural environment stabilized to some degree. Ríos Montt's inefficient and erratic governing style, accompanied by his born-again Christianity in a predominantly Catholic country, resulted in his replacement by Brigadier General Oscar Mejía Víctores in 1983. The strategy for conducting the war continued largely unchanged.

Judged on its own terms, Guatemala's counterinsurgency war was very successful. Guatemala City and much of the countryside is now pacified. As recently as 1982, the capital was like an armed camp, periodically racked by terrorist explosions. Within miles of the city, guerrillas controlled large areas of the country, stopping cars, issuing travel passes, and collecting revolutionary taxes. The guerrillas, once 4,000 strong, have been reduced to between 1,200 and 2,000 and are concentrated in the border provinces near Mexico. The lessened security risk and a renewed concern for Guatemala's international image led in 1984 and 1985 to relative reductions in political killings and "disappearances" (from a high of about 500 political murders a month, mostly by the right, to about 100 a month in 1984–85) and to elections resulting in civilian rule. By 1988 the civilian government of Vinicio Cerezo had persuaded most observers that human rights conditions had improved, but heated debate continued over whether they had improved enough, and over the failure to punish past human rights violators.

As Guatemala has stabilized and undergone a transition to civilian rule, the United States has indicated its readiness to resume military and economic aid to the country. The leaders of Guatemala's 40,200-strong army disdain advice from a country that lost its first sustained guerrilla war in Vietnam and is restrained by public opinion from waging Guatemala-style warfare. But the army's civic action programs and "model villages" require economic assistance that the declining Guatemalan economy cannot provide.

Now that the guerrilla challenge has been turned back once more, NSAs argue that the United States can renew assistance without compromising itself too badly. HRAs are troubled by the nagging question of whether "victory" Guatemala-style will become the model for U.S. policy elsewhere in the region where military defeat of guerrillas is the ultimate objective.

Question: Will U.S. Military and Economic Assistance Strengthen the Apparent Democratic Opening in Guatemala or Will It Encourage a Mere Democratic Facade?

Discussion:

The coup attempt in May 1988 of military officers and civilian elites opposed to the government of Vinicio Cerezo produced a necessary realism about the prospects for democratic rule in Guatemala. Debates about the amount of change that has occurred in Guatemala and the appropriate U.S. response are classic examples of opposing sides seeing the same glass of water as being half full or half empty.

NSAs see the glass as half full and emphasize the positive aspects of recent changes. The United States gave $2.4 million in military assistance and $174 million in economic aid to Guatemala in 1987 and has requested $7.6 million in military aid and $142 million in economic aid for 1988. NSAs argue that the critical moment has arrived when military aid and the training of Guatemalan police can reinforce democratic progress in Guatemala. As was demonstrated by loyalist elements of the army under Defense Minister Hector Gramajo, who put down the coup attempt in May 1988, the majority of the military backs civilian rule. Their efforts to defend Guatemalan liberty should be rewarded and recognized by U.S. policy. Such aid will also help the army prosecute the war against the guerrillas more effectively, ending guerrilla sabotage of the economy and the human rights abuses attributable to guerrilla operations.

HRAs point out that, given their pride in having won a guerrilla war without U.S. help and their belief that the human rights strings attached to U.S. aid could restrain future conduct, Guatemala's military leaders are not overly eager to embrace the U.S. offer of assistance. They need aid to finance their "model village" program, but will resist strictures on the manner in which they wish to conduct the counterinsurgency campaign. The Guatemalan army remains, like its counterpart in Honduras, the power behind the civilian throne. HRAs emphasize this fact when insisting that the United States distance itself from a system that has been among the cruelest in Central America. In their view, recent developments in Guatemala are more appearance than reality. To renew U.S. aid at this time would be to signal the generals that a democratic facade is all that is needed to please external opinion while allowing the military to solidify its hold over the country without promoting basic political and economic reforms. Those reforms include a definitive end to current human rights violations, the prosecution of past offenders, and civilian control of rural development programs.

In the flawed and morally ambiguous world in which the NSA believes the United States must operate, the relatively positive developments in Guatemala provide the opportunity for the United States to regain influence with a strategic regional actor. This influence can be used to reinforce democratic developments in the country and to encourage Guatemala to align its views of Nicaragua and the Central American peace process more closely with those of the United States.

Note

1. These publications are available to the public from S/LPD Room 5917, U.S. Department of State, Washington, DC 20530. *Comandante Bayardo Arce's Secret Speech before the Nicaraguan Socialist Party* (1984); *The U.S. and Central America: Implementing the National Bipartisan Commission Report* (August 1986); *Human Rights in Nicaragua under the Sandinistas* (December 1986); *Nicaragua: The Moral and Strategic Stakes* (February 1987); *Democracy in Latin America and the Caribbean: The Promise and the Challenge* (March 1987); *A Plan for Fully Funding the Recommendations of the National Bipartisan Commission on Central America* (March 1987); *Central America: What are the Alternatives?* (April 1987); *Negotiations in Central America* (October 1987); *The Guerrilla Movement in El Salvador* (July 1987); *Nicaragua's Interior Ministry: Instrument of Political Consolidation* (August 1987); *Nicaraguan Biographies: A Resource Book* (January 1988).

4

The Politics of Central American Policy

We're not only poorly informed but confused and divided. . . . Unfortunately, the debate over Central America has become polarized.

—Bill Moyers, CBS News, 1982

This is an astounding fact. After six years of debate and discussion and evening television news, only 38 percent of the American people know which side [in Nicaragua] the Administration is supporting.

—House Minority Leader Robert H. Michel (R-Il.), contra aid debate, 1986

During the course of the 1980s Central America became the first foreign policy issue since Vietnam to divide North Americans profoundly along political lines. Terrorism, the Arab-Israeli conflict, apartheid—none of these highly charged issues that occupied the front pages of newspapers polarized opinion and preoccupied government like Central America. The reasons for the emergence of Central America as the most debated foreign policy issue for the majority of the Reagan years are many. Some concern the nature of the Reagan presidency itself, but others are about changes in the way government makes foreign policy, shifts in public sentiment about U.S. involvement overseas, and the opening up of the foreign policy–making process to new actors.

As the quotes from Bill Moyers and Bob Michel indicate, the

intense debate about Central America among politicians, activists, and policymakers took place against a backdrop of significant public ignorance about Central America. For most of this period of intense media attention on Central America, polling data continued to show that only about one-fourth of those asked could identify which side the United States supported in El Salvador and Nicaragua. On the other hand, some of the same polls indicated consistent opposition to administration policy toward Central America, particularly funding for the Nicaraguan contras, by two to one margins for much of the 1980s. How can it be that citizens were at once divided in their opinions, ignorant of the basic facts about Central American policy, and frequently opposed to the administration's policy?

The Public and Policy

Because the United States is a representative democracy, elected officials must be generally responsive to voters' opinions to be reelected. But the degree to which the voting public devotes attention to government policy in general and to foreign policy in particular varies greatly.

Public opinion specialists talk about three different types of publics: the mass public, the attentive public, and opinion makers. The mass public, estimated at 75 percent of the population, is said to be generally uninterested and uninformed about foreign policy issues unless their own lives are directly affected by something happening overseas (as in the case of Vietnam, where losing a child in the war often motivated parents to become more politically aware). The second public is the attentive public, that 5 percent of the population that remains active and well-informed on foreign policy issues. Within this attentive public is a small group of opinion makers who often play leadership roles in their communities and who help to shape the opinions of their fellow citizens. Some 20 percent of the population is apolitical and virtually indifferent to any policy concerns.

The mass public, as the polls about knowledge of Central America may indicate, has not become very involved in the debate over Central America. As with the Vietnam war, individuals whose lives were in some way touched by the conflicts in Central America—

through travel to the region or contact with a refugee sponsored by their church or synagogue—were sometimes mobilized to become active on the Central American issue. (See Box, "The Churches and Central America," pp. 140–43.) But most members of the mass public were what public opinion experts call "inattentive" to Central America. The "inattentive public" is predisposed against U.S. involvement in other countries' affairs unless a clear and compelling issue of national interest and national security can be demonstrated to be at stake. These views of the inattentive public may explain an important part of the opposition to aid to the contras (which varied during the 1980s from 40 percent to 70 percent, depending on the wording of the question and the timing of the poll) and the extensive "public relations" efforts of the administration to show that "vital interests" of the United States were threatened in Central America.

The attentive public and opinion makers include local and national elected officials, religious leaders, journalists, and academics. Many are members of community organizations such as the Jaycees, Women's Club, and Rotary Club, as well as foreign policy and world affairs councils, or religious and ethnic organizations. Some may belong to organizations which have national offices that try to affect the policy debate in Washington. The interest and influence of these associations varies from issue to issue and from group to group. The attentive public and opinion makers have been the source of most of the heat and some of the light generated by the Central America debate.

Members of the attentive public and opinion makers make conflicting claims about the support that exists among the general public for the policies of the Reagan administration toward Central America. Those opposed to administration policy cite the numerous surveys extending over many years that show consistent pluralities and sometimes strong majorities against contra aid. Proponents of administration policy point to equally consistent survey results that the general public strongly opposes the development of a Communist state in Central America. They argue that lack of knowledge of the true nature of the Sandinistas is the reason for opposition to contra aid.

In an attempt to get at the deeper sentiments behind these polling results, the Roosevelt Center conducted a series of "focus

THE CHURCHES AND CENTRAL AMERICA

Lamp store owner Jerry McBrayer, a North Carolina Republican and early supporter of President Reagan, had never questioned U.S. assistance to the contras before traveling to Nicaragua with a church group three years ago.

McBrayer, 54, an Episcopalian, saw women and children living in shacks without water one block from his hotel in downtown Managua. He saw cinderblock houses going up along the road to the airport—evidence that, for some, life was getting better. He talked at length to everyone he met, and he came back a changed man.

"It's not cut and dried," he said.

Arming the contras to fight the Sandinista regime would not end the war in Nicaragua, he told the Lions Club and church groups in his native Morgantown. Negotiations among countries in the region might. "We don't need to kill women and children," McBrayer said in an interview last week. "This thing has got to stop."

With those words, McBrayer joined a coalition of mainline Protestants, Catholics and Jews who in the last five years have been the loudest and most consistent critics of the Reagan administration's policy of military intervention in Central America, according to members of Congress, lobbyists and spokesmen for the administration.

Not since the waning days of the Vietnam war have mainstream churchgoers become galvanized around a foreign policy issue to that extent, church leaders say.

A legislative newsletter called Impact '88, sponsored by 17 Protestant, Catholic and Jewish groups and focused on the upcoming congressional campaigns, is blunt: "For Americans, the number one moral problem of this decade is public policy in Central America."

The impact these churches have had on U.S. policy is hard to measure, but foreign policy analysts say it is undeniable that by stirring up and sustaining public rejection of military intervention, they have restrained the president in what he was willing to propose and Congress in what it was willing to finance.

"They have made it much more difficult for Reagan to pursue the policy of unrestrained military escalation he advocated early on," said William M. LeoGrande, political science professor at American University.

Drawing on years of work in Central American missions, a grass-roots constituency in the United States and an unusually unified moral position, these religious organizations have helped turn some members of Congress around and helped defeat others.

Cindy Buhl, director of the political action committee Pax Americas, credits churches and church-affiliated groups with helping whittle the list of congressional swing votes on Central America—from about 80 House votes in 1984 to about 30 now and from approximately 16 in the Senate four years ago to 5 now. "They organized early and best," she said.

The religious lobby's presence was felt during recent House discussions on contra aid. "They've lobbied on other issues, but on this one I really saw the impact," said George Kundanis, floor assistant to Rep. Thomas S. Foley (D-Wash.), who helped the majority leader engineer Democratic alternatives. "Conservative constituents picked this issue out as different."

"I don't know of a single foreign policy issue on which they've weighed in more heavily," said Rep. Henry J. Hyde (R-Ill.), a Reagan supporter. "It has been a clerical full-court press. They were particularly effective in marginal districts."

Rep. Dave McCurdy (D-Okla.) from Norman, one of those marginal districts, was "definitely lobbied more on Central America than on any other issue," said legislative assistant Mike Chapman. His constituents are split on military aid for the contras, Chapman said, "but all the church groups were saying no aid, no aid." On Feb. 3, McCurdy voted against Reagan's last attempt at lethal aid for the contras.

Clearly, other factors have influenced members such as McCurdy, notably the progress of the peace plan proposed by Costa Rican President Oscar Arias. Yet few in Congress deny that each side wanted the churches' help, particularly because every vote was close.

When the Democratic leadership was putting together its fragile, $30.8 million package of humanitarian aid for Nicaragua last month, Rep. David R. Obey (D-Wis.) called on the U.S. Catholic Conference, the policy-making body of Catholic bishops, for support.

The Democratic caucus staff gave members of Congress a list of organizations supporting or opposing the proposal, which began, "Due to the interest of many members in the positions of peace and religious organizations on the Democratic package. . . ."

Church groups split over the plan, breaking a pattern of unity. All but five GOP members voted against it, and the plan failed, 208 to 216.

One reason churches have been persuasive, said LeoGrande, is that "they've been able to ask the moral questions." Policy-makers tend to ask "Will it work, is it in the national interest and can we sustain it politically?" LeoGrande said. What they need to hear is, "Is what we're doing in Central America right?"

Other issues reflecting moral values, including abortion, have pitted Catholics against mainline Protestants and split Protestant ranks. But

Central America has drawn them together: Catholics, Episcopalians, Friends, Lutherans, Presbyterians, American Baptists, Church of the Brethren, Unitarians, United Methodists and the United Church of Christ. Mainstream Jews have played a smaller role, mostly through the Union of American Hebrew Congregations.

Representatives of those groups say Central American problems are rooted principally in poverty and longstanding denial of human rights, not simply in Communist infiltration. Those problems should be resolved by Latin American countries, not by a Cold War struggle between the United States and the Soviet Union, they say.

Religious leaders first made a moral argument against military intervention in Central America in late 1979 when President Carter proposed $5 million for the right-wing El Salvador government. But their congregations were looking for practical as well as moral reasons. Eventually churchgoers came to believe that money spent on guns abroad could better be spent repairing the American economy, that money appropriated by Congress was not going where it was intended and that the United States shouldn't be drawn into another Vietnam.

Mary Hayes Holmes, a Presbyterian from North Carolina, traveled to Managua in April 1983, "not knowing the difference between Nicaragua and Nigeria." She returned believing "we should leave those people alone. We're not Big Brother." Holmes joined the Carolinas Interfaith Task Force on Central America, one of about 300 such groups nationwide.

Church groups are taken more seriously on Central America than on other issues because they speak from firsthand experience in the region, said Kirk O'Donnell, president of the Center for National Policy, a Democratic think tank. Visits by U.S. Catholics and Protestants multiplied after the murder of Archbishop Oscar Romero in El Salvador in March 1980 and the death of four American nuns in December of that year. One organization alone, Witness for Peace, has sent 3,000 volunteers to Nicaragua, according to an ecumenical newsletter.

Those believers often show more passion than some policy-makers are comfortable with. But intense feeling is what keeps many activists from giving up against what seem insurmountable odds, says Sister Marlene Bertke, a Benedictine nun from Erie, Pa. The poor "are our brothers and sisters, and our country is working against the Gospel," says Bertke, 56, who visited Nicaragua in 1984 and El Salvador in 1986.

Churches send millions of dollars in aid to Central America. Catholic Relief Services, for example, sends about $3.6 million in food and development asssistance every year; Church World Service, the development arm of the Protestants' National Council of Churches, has provided more than $1 million since spring 1986.

In this country, church efforts on Central American issues are significant. Since 1983, George Chauncey, a member of a four-member Washington lobbying staff for the Presbyterian Church-USA, has worked on nothing else. Three of the 12 members of the United Methodists' Washington staff spend part of their time on Central America. So do four persons working for the U.S. Catholic Conference.

The Catholic bishops keep more than six feet of files on Central America at their Massachusetts Avenue headquarters. From 1979 to 1984, according to one of those files, the bishops testified 10 times before Congress and made about 30 other public statements on Central America.

Representatives of the religious right who support the administration have spent comparatively little time on Central American issues, and most of that monitoring the mainline churches. They accuse those churches of contributing resources to Marxist operations and prolonging the conflict.

McBrayer doesn't see a problem with such cooperation if it will raise the standard of living in the region. As he drove to work last week, McBrayer said, he began wondering whether a Georgia organization called Habitat, which builds houses for poor people, couldn't do work in Nicaragua. "Maybe," he added, "with a little help from the Soviets?"

—Laura Sessions Stepp
(*Washington Post,*
April 14, 1988)

groups" in six cities across the United States in the summer of 1986.[1] The focus group results revealed a complicated and contradictory picture of public attitudes, encouraging to neither opponents nor supporters of Reagan administration policy.[2] Faced with a stark choice of sending U.S. troops to overthrow the Sandinistas, supporting a native rebellion (the contras), or doing nothing, small majorities of focus group participants favored contra aid. But this support was extremely fragile, based on very poor information about Central America, and accompanied by a great deal of skepticism about the democratic nature of the contras. While participants were indeed concerned about Soviet influence in Central America, they responded positively to a hypothetical scenario in which an armed group came to power in a poor Central American country and expropriated land and other property to benefit a poor majority, a scenario which some would argue corresponds to the Sandinistas.

The picture that emerged from these focus groups was of a public deeply traumatized by the Vietnam experience and skeptical of any policy that required the use of U.S. forces. They were concerned about Communism less in the abstract as an ideological threat than as embodied in a direct Soviet presence in the hemisphere that clearly threatened the U.S. mainland. Given their perception of Central America as a poor region marked by tremendous inequalities of wealth and power and by violent politics, they were willing to support quite radical reform measures that promised to address the needs of this poor majority. Most striking was the administration's apparent inability to convince this public of the case for connections between the Sandinistas, the Soviets, and security threats to the United States.

Critics and supporters of Reagan administration policy toward Central America were sensitive to this public component of their battles over policy. A 1982 "Summary Paper" on Central America policy from the National Security Council stated:

> We continue to have serious difficulties with U.S. public and Congressional opinion, which jeopardizes our ability to stay the course.
> Decision: That, under the auspices of the White House, the public information effort be augmented and targeted on improving communication with the Congress and with opinion leaders.

In early 1983 President Reagan authorized the setting up of White House and State Department offices to coordinate this effort. The "White House Outreach Group on Central America" sponsored weekly seminars on Central American issues for hand-selected representatives of groups largely supportive of administration policy. The Outreach Group also encouraged the publication of articles and advertisements and the placement of "op-eds" in major newspapers arguing the correctness and urgency of the administration's case. Also in 1983, the State Department established an "Office of Public Diplomacy for Latin America and the Caribbean." The office issued official documents making the case for administration policy and staffed the numerous requests for administration spokespersons in debates on Central American policy. Both of the offices would later be criticized by Congress for violating prohibitions against "lobbying and disseminating government information for publicity and progaganda purposes."

Is the Message Skewed?

Because of the role the media play in shaping public perceptions, both critics and supporters of administration policy during the 1980s debated the impact of media coverage of Central America. Most discussions of the media and Central America tend to focus on the supposed bias of coverage of events in the region. On El Salvador the ideological tilt of media critics underwent a complete reversal. In the early 1980s, the strongest criticism of the media came from the right. Correspondents such as Raymond Bonner of the *New York Times* and Karen DeYoung of the *Washington Post* were charged with "serving the guerrilla cause," "engaging in disinformation," and unfairly introducing the "Vietnam syndrome" into their coverage of El Salvador.

By the late 1980s, the criticism had come full circle. The North American Congress on Latin America (NACLA), a research organization opposed to Reagan administration policy in Central America, published an article in the summer of 1986 titled "Whitewashing Duarte." The article argued that U.S. reporters who were once skeptical of official policy in El Salvador had become ". . . a chorus singing the praise of Administration policy. . . ."[3]

Some examples of the accusations leveled against the press are worth citing. In "Whitewashing Duarte," author Marc Cooper, a free-lance journalist who did a 1984 *Playboy* interview with President Duarte, states his central conclusion:

> An analysis of more than 800 articles taken from *The New York Times*, the *Los Angeles Times*, *The Washington Post*, *The Christian Science Monitor* and *The Miami Herald* stretching from March 1984 through October 1985, reveals that the Salvador story was no longer being reported as one of repression, escalating war and massive human rights violations, but rather as one of hope for peace and democratic renaissance.

Cooper offers a number of explanations for this change in the nature of the reporting from El Salvador—except the possibility that conditions in El Salvador itself might have changed. One of the most revealing explanations is what he refers to as the "God That Failed Syndrome," in which veteran correspondents

> romanticize the guerrillas as possessing all those human qualities—mercy, compassion, reason and sensitivity—that apparently were lacking among the government forces. . . .
>
> And once the guerrillas had failed to live up to the impossible standards set for them by some U.S. reporters, the insurgents found themselves villainized in a flow of articles over the last year from reporters ending their tour of Salvador. The decades-long history of insurgency and counter-insurgency has been neatly collapsed into the facile and supremely cynical conclusion that both sides—Army and guerrillas—are basically the same.

This implies that journalists did—as many conservatives believe—have a naive identification with the left in El Salvador that unfairly influenced their coverage. Initially, such naivete benefited the guerrillas by portraying them as the side wearing white hats. When guerrilla tactics shifted in response to their changing strategic position in El Salvador, they were revealed as not having a monopoly on virtue and, subsequently, vilified by disillusioned reporters. Cooper's own analysis, if it were correct, would confirm the charge of poor journalistic standards directed at several of these journalists.

Press coverage of Central America did evolve over the course of the 1980s. In the case of El Salvador this may be because, as conservative journalist Daniel James concludes,

> a growing public awareness that the media's reporting on El Salvador had suffered from bias, and a corresponding realization among some journalists and editors that that was not only wrong but hurting the profession, has resulted in some correction of their Salvadoran coverage.[4]

Or it may be that "ideological pressure" from the right wing has exacted its toll, as Marc Cooper argues.

But other factors also help to explain why a different story has come out of El Salvador in the mid-1980s. First, the nature of the conflict changed. The human costs of the war went down in terms of death squad murders, but civilian casualties increased with shifts in guerrilla tactics to selective terror and economic sabotage and in government tactics to "sweeps," aerial bombardment, and forced "rescues" or relocations of peasants from guerrilla areas.

Second, these changes were underreported, for understandable but not always defensible reasons. There were attempts by government officials to limit accurate coverage. The Salvadoran armed forces developed a "public relations" department, Coprefa, which billed itself as a news source, but could more accurately be seen as an "agit-prop" organ. Its influence on journalists and ability to control the news increased. Attempts by U.S. embassy and Salvadoran government personnel to limit reporters' access to combat zones, particularly to areas subject to bombing, discouraged "on-the-scene" coverage of the newest victims of the war.

Another explanation for decreased coverage is that while El Salvador may be in more trouble than the administration would like to admit, it did not face between 1984 and 1986 the threat of collapse or a guerrilla takeover, as it did at the height of U.S. coverage. For this reason, many news organs, and especially financially pressed television networks, reduced the number of correspondents based in El Salvador and/or moved their bureau chiefs to Managua or back to Miami. Editors, reflecting what they perceived to be declining reader interest, did not feature so many stories on Central America. If the decline of the "middle option's" fortunes (as indicated by the 1988 defeat of the Christian Democrats) continues, El Salvador could well return to the front pages again.

This "here today, gone tomorrow" nature of press attention is, unfortunately, characteristic of the way the United States receives information about the rest of the world. But it does not appear to reflect the ideological capitulation of the news media to the administration line nor "corrections" of earlier lapses in sound journalistic practices. News coverage of any event, from a local PTA meeting to a murky struggle in Central America, is never a completely accurate portrayal of real events, but is at any given moment only a rough approximation of what is actually happening. That approximation in Central America appears to be about as accurate (or inaccurate) now as it was at the beginning of the Central American crisis in the late 1970s. However, the "truth," to the degree it can ever be known, became less pleasing to the left and more pleasing to the right in El Salvador during the course of the 1980s. In the early 1980s the media covered the highly repressive nature of the military-civilian junta and the popular base of guerrilla support, two stories that the right did not want to hear. In the mid-1980s the media documented a decline in the appalling level of death squad activity and the turnout of millions of Salvadorans to vote under the guns of the guerrillas, a message unwelcome to those who saw Duarte as heading a sham democracy. By the late 1980s El Salvador was again the object of more intense coverage that may ignite a new round of media criticism.

Press coverage of Nicaragua in the 1980s has affected the policy debate in the United States by conveying two basic messages: the Sandinistas are serious revolutionaries who do not have a Western-style democracy in mind for Nicaragua, and the opposition contras have a command structure dominated by arch-conservatives and former National Guardsmen and have been militarily ineffective and politically disorganized. Foreign policy elites who do not agree with one or the other of these messages have mounted campaigns to change what they choose to call "mistaken perceptions" about the "truth" in Nicaragua.

Supporters and critics of official policy remain focused on media coverage because of its important influence on attitudes toward Central America. But the extreme—and apparently justified—skepticism with which many in the news media greeted the official Washington version of Nicaraguan "incursions" into Honduras in 1986 and 1988 is a final confirmation that the media is not completely captive to any single perspective on Central America.

Congress and Central America: A House Divided

The domestic division over Vietnam generated a foreign-policy assertiveness by Congress, resulting in new laws prohibiting the President's powers to commit U.S. troops to war without Congressional approval (the War Powers Act), and providing for increased oversight of intelligence operations. The hostility between the executive and legislative branches over Central America took place within this context and was surrounded by debate over whether Congress, in the wake of Vietnam, had exceeded its constitutional role in affecting policy through control of the "purse strings." Former Secretary of State Henry Kissinger forcefully argued that the United States was approaching deadlock in its foreign policy–making process:

> The real issue is not whether [administration] officials are entitled to substitute their judgment for that of Congress—not even the most zealous White House staffer would

claim that—but whether our system of checks and balances is moving excessively toward the former with ever less concern for balance between the coequal branches of government. Nearly insoluble constitutional and personal dilemmas arise when each branch of government acts on the premise that the other is producing disaster and must be thwarted at all costs.

The foundation for Congressional opposition to Reagan administration policy in Central America had been laid before the 1980 election. Although President Carter is often credited with establishing human rights as a cornerstone of U.S. foreign policy, he was in some ways following the lead of prior Congressional action. A group of liberal lawmakers, the so-called "Watergate generation," had come to Washington in the mid-1970s with an international agenda of human rights and support for reform in the Third World, and a suspicion of the CIA and what they viewed as U.S. interventionism. Representatives Michael Barnes (D-Md.) and Gerry Studds (D-Mass.) and Senators Tom Harkin (D-Iowa) and Christopher Dodd (D-Ct.) were members of this group who later would take a leadership role in opposition to the Reagan administration's policies in Central America.

The landslide election of Ronald Reagan and the attendant loss of a Democratic majority in the Senate shifted the terms of the debate on Central America. The 1980 Republican Party platform had identified Central America as a place where Communist advances could be "rolled back." This was the earliest version of what came to be known as the Reagan Doctrine, a policy of support for armed groups seeking to overthrow regimes linked to the Soviet Union and its allies. Secretary of State Alexander Haig wanted to "draw the line" against Communism in Central America and "go to the source" in seeking to undermine the Sandinistas, a reference that many understood to be a veiled threat to Cuba. Confronting a "final offensive" in El Salvador by leftist guerrillas and an increasingly radical Nicaragua, the administration took steps early in 1981 to increase dramatically military aid to El Salvador, authorize CIA covert operations in Central America, and fund efforts by Argentinian military advisers to train an anti-Sandinista exile army.

The result was a firestorm of protest over administration policy in El Salvador and a delayed, but also intense, criticism of Nicaragua policy. Congress, fueled by vocal support from human rights constituencies, succeeded in imposing constraints on the administration that led one conservative critic to complain that the Reagan administration's policy in El Salvador was "not very different from that of its predecessor":

It [the Reagan Administration] too now acknowledged that—whatever the role of Cubans, Nicaraguans, or others—there were domestic causes of disorder in El Salvador. It too called for an improvement in the human rights performance of the Salvadoran government and armed forces, and—to the dismay and even disgust of its more conservative supporters at home—it supported the land reform program, which in El Salvador had expropriated the 350 largest holdings, destined for conversion into cooperatives.[5]

The reasons for the change in or, for some conservatives, defeat of administration approaches to El Salvador were multiple. Mounting and well-publicized human rights violations by death squads with acknowledged ties to government security forces mobilized human rights groups in the United States. The murder of four North American churchwomen by members of the Salvadoran National Guard captured the attention of ordinary citizens and established in the minds of many the innocence of the victims and the guilt of the U.S.-supported government.

Because El Salvador's was an overt, not covert, war, Congressional approval for funding of the war effort was crucial to administration policy. And so, over time, the administration had to adopt many of Congress's goals for El Salvador: support for the reformist Duarte and reform policies, including such measures as land reform, the nationalization of the banking sector and foreign trade, and calling attention to massive human rights abuses by the Salvadoran armed forces with legislation that made aid contingent on human rights progress. Rather than choosing the "lesser evil" of authoritarian regimes, the administration joined with Congress in promoting democratic practices as the best defense against Communist insurgency. This compromise disappointed both national security analysts, who believed that the most important U.S. goal was the military defeat of the guerrilla forces, and human rights activists, who opposed any U.S. complicity in the continuing repression. But it was key to creating a sustainable policy and high levels of funding for the remainder of the administration's tenure.

Executive–legislative branch relations regarding Nicaragua produced not compromise but escalating conflict. Because the war against Nicaragua was originally "covert," Congressional funding was for some time not as crucial, as public, or as massive as it was for El Salvador. Most observers also agree that until the Iran-contra affair and the signing of the Esquipulas II peace agreement, the administration consistently set the terms of the debate with Congress on Nicaragua. With greater effectiveness than for El Salvador, supporters of official policy could threaten to charge those in opposition to administration policy with having "lost" Nicaragua to Communism. Nicaragua's military ties to the Soviet Union and Cuba, speeches by Sandinista leaders in favor of a Marxist political system, and their attacks on political opponents, made most members of Congress uncomfortable opposing administration approaches when they could not offer a positive alternative. The human rights abuses by the U.S.-backed government in El Salvador had embarrassed the administration and emboldened Congressional opposition, while human rights violations by the contras were never as massive or as publicly embarrassing as those by the death squads in El Salvador. And the Sandinistas themselves were charged with antidemocratic behavior such as improper imprisonment of opponents, abusive interrogation practices, and outright "disappearances" in the Miskito area of Nicaragua.

These different relations between Congress and the administration on Nicaragua led to what Republican critics on the Iran-contra committees condemned as a mixed message on contra aid. From 1981 to 1988 the Congress reversed its position on aid to the contras at least six times. Twenty to twenty-five "swing" votes in the House of Representatives, both Democrats and Republicans, held the power to advance or defeat administration proposals. The direction of the "swings" depended on the members' reaction to events in Nicaragua and in Washington, and to the particular formulation of contra aid presented. Congress denied aid and approved aid under varying conditions and restrictions, in protracted and exhausting battles with the administration, and under the gun of public lobbying on all sides of the issue.

For its part, the administration shifted its rationale for the different forms of pressure it sought to exert on the Sandinistas. The contras were originally funded to interdict arms supplies to the Salvadoran guerrillas and not to overthrow the Nicaraguan government, a proposition advocated by the contras, but prohibited, for a time, by the Boland (D-Mass.) amendment. Later the official goal of the policy was to bring the Sandinistas to the negotiating table, and still later to force democratic change inside Nicaragua. While

President Reagan spoke of the Nicaraguan rebels' need "to have their way and take over" if the Sandinistas did not "cry uncle," official spokespersons always denied that overthrow of the regime was the administration's ultimate intention.

Former Secretary of State Kissinger recognized that the administration's real objective had been the "overthrow of the Sandinista political structure," and argued that Congressional restrictions had prevented the achievement of this goal. Senator Bill Bradley (D-N.J.), a contra aid supporter for several years, allocated the blame differently in explaining his vote in 1988 against contra aid:

> I blame Ronald Reagan. There is a difference between speeches that rail at communists and a policy that effectively counters them. Speeches are easy, policy takes effort and care. Yet, after seven years, people still don't know whether Reagan wants to overthrow the Sandinistas or get them to negotiate. Not knowing the ends, Congress has understandably resisted authorizing the means.

The disputes between Congress and the executive branch were more than items of interest for journalists and pundits "inside the Beltway." With President Reagan personally determined not to let another Communist state be installed during his term in office, Nicaragua remained at the top of the administration's foreign policy agenda. Key administration members, including the President, were convinced that what happened in Central America was of vital interest to the United States. When Congress defeated contra aid in May 1984, the administration launched an ambitious campaign to continue aid by other means and to reverse public and Congressional opposition. The pursuit of the first of these twin goals led the administration into the ethical and legal thicket known as the Iran-contra affair, the details of which have been discussed elsewhere (see box, "Iran-Contra: An Affair to Remember," pp. 54–59). The pursuit of the second led to White House orchestration of an impressive network of conservative activist groups, whose development paralleled the pre-existing activist organizations opposing administration policy.

The Central American Apple of Discord

When then–Secretary of State Alexander Haig spoke in the early days of the Reagan administration of "drawing the line" against

Soviet expansionism in Central America, and attempted to define what was happening in El Salvador as "part of the global Communist campaign coordinated by Havana and Moscow," he and other conservatives were surprised by the strength and sources of public opposition to these policies. What one conservative dubbed the "clerico-left" lobby of opposition to Reagan administration policies includes an impressive array of elements of the coalition that opposed the Vietnam War, and current members of religious, feminist, antinuclear, pro-environment, and other liberal movements. A Directory of Central American Organizations published by the Central American Resource Center of Austin, Texas, in 1987 lists over 1,000 entities that educate, lobby, or organize action on Central America. Largely funded by individual contributions and lacking the high-level endorsement available to pro-administration groups, the left/liberal lobbies have turned conviction, experience, and persistence into powerful tools to influence debate over Central American policy in the United States.

The roster of activist groups opposed to Reagan administration policy includes the so-called "solidarity groups" such as the Nicaragua Network, the Committee in Solidarity with the People of El Salvador (CISPES), and the Network in Solidarity with the People of Guatemala (NISGUA). In each of these cases the groups have local chapters that are coordinated by national offices located in Washington, D.C. Their solidarity is with that political movement which they believe represents the "people": the Sandinista government in Nicaragua, the FDR-FMLN in El Salvador, and the URNG (Guatemalan National Revolutionary Unity) and its civilian allies in Guatemala.

Also active on the Central American issue are several kinds of volunteer brigades that organize trips for North Americans to the region. Some offer particular skills such as TECNICA, the group that sponsored Benjamin Linder, the young Washington state engineer killed by contra forces in the remote village where he was constructing hydroelectric facilities. Others encourage average citizens to experience Central America in delegations that may visit the region for days or weeks.

Church groups are among the most organized and active. Denominations that have made Central America a major moral concern for their members are: Catholics, Episcopalians, Quakers,

Lutherans, Presbyterians, American Baptists, Church of the Brethren, Unitarian Universalists, United Methodists, and the United Church of Christ. Elements within the churches such as the Sanctuary Movement, which sponsors Central American refugees seeking political asylum in the United States, or Witness for Peace, which has sent thousands of volunteer observers into war zones, have been involved in acts of civil disobedience to press their opposition to government policies.

In the nation's capital are numerous institutes, research centers, and lobbying organizations that address different aspects of the Central American debate. Some, such as the Washington Office on Latin America, are supported by coalitions of church and labor groups and focus directly on the policymaking process in Washington.

Votes on contra aid were times of intense lobbying and political activities by groups hoping to defeat all aid. *Countdown 1987* was one group formed during the summer of 1987 to coordinate and unify the work of the numerous groups opposed to contra aid. Formed by long-time left/liberal activists and funders, *Countdown* followed a sophisticated, campaign-type format. Rosa De Lauro, a long-time Democratic party activist and former aide to Democratic Senator Christopher Dodd, was recruited as director.

Countdown's strategy was to single out House and Senate "swing" districts where they felt they had a reasonable chance of garnering a "no" vote on Reagan's contra aid request. The group organized a local presence in the districts. At the local level the work consisted of phone banking to constituents, door to door canvassing, public forums on the issue, and other grass roots organizing techniques. At the national level *Countdown's* work involved lobbying Congress (through an allied political action committee or PAC), coordinating with other organizations in their anti–contra aid coalition, joint strategizing with allies on the Hill, conducting a study of public opinion regarding contra aid, and producing anti–contra aid commercials that aired in the swing districts. They also encouraged academics and public figures opposed to aid to write op-eds or otherwise speak out on the issue.

Close contact and common strategies and tactics were maintained with allies in the House and Senate, including Speaker

Wright, Majority Whip Tony Coelho (D-Calif.), Deputy Majority Whip (and coordinator of the House Nicaragua Task Force) David Bonior (D-Miss.), and Senators Kennedy, Dodd, and Harkin.

Because of their outspoken opposition to administration policy and their sympathy for revolutionary causes in Central America, several of the solidarity groups came under the scrutiny of government security agencies. On the grounds that CISPES constituted a "national security" threat, the FBI planted informers within the organization, photographed files and people at demonstrations, and carried out surveillance of members. The investigation continued for five years and involved more than one hundred groups, including the Maryknoll Sisters and the United Auto Workers.

Executive assistant director of the investigation Oliver B. Revell, acknowledged in Congressional testimony that "we may have seen some wavering over that line" between a legitimate investigation and political spying. He argued, however, that there was a legal basis for the probe: circumstantial evidence collected in 1983 that CISPES members were sending money to the FMLN in El Salvador. The FBI classifies the FMLN as a terrorist organization and suspects them of bombings in Washington in 1983–84.

The investigation failed to lead to any indictments of CISPES members or to gather any evidence of criminal wrongdoing on the part of CISPES. Congressional committees initiated a probe to determine whether the FBI's actions were politically motivated, especially since they continued for years without producing any evidence of illegality.

The administration's attempt to swing public and Congressional opinion behind its policies confronted a number of obstacles, as well as benefiting from the advantages of having control of the executive branch of government. President Reagan made extensive use of what Teddy Roosevelt called the "bully pulpit" of presidential speechmaking. President Reagan gave an unparalleled number of addresses to joint sessions of Congress on Central America, and rarely missed an opportunity in his opening statements at press conferences to make reference to the current manifestation of the Central American debate confronting Congress. Through the State Department's Office of Public Diplomacy, White House briefings for visiting delegations of citizens, and the activities of conservative "think tanks" and research institutions, the administration pressed its case against the Sandinistas and for its policies in every forum available to it.

The administration's "selling" of its Central America policy was also intended to operate within several restraints. One was self-imposed: in late 1981 President Reagan signed Executive Order 12333, which prohibited the Central Intelligence Agency from engaging in activities "to influence United States political processes, public opinion, policies or media." Another came from Congress: statutory prohibition against the use of Congressionally appropriated funds to ". . . influence in any manner a Member of Congress." These prohibitions against domestic use of the CIA and executive branch intrusion in the Congressional political process proved difficult to abide by. William Casey, CIA director and close confidant of the President, was allegedly involved in every aspect of the administration's selling of Central America. Reports from the House Foreign Affairs Committee charged that the Office of Public Diplomacy hired public relations firms to carry out propaganda activities legally prohibited to the Executive branch.

Indeed, the Iran-contra hearings in Congress uncovered an interlocking directorate of private firms, public charities, and lobbying groups orchestrated by Colonel Oliver North on behalf of administration policy. One illustration is International Business Communications (IBC), a public relations firm owned by Frank Gomez and Richard Miller. Before the cut-off of contra aid in 1984, IBC received noncompetitive contracts from the Office of Public Diplomacy to publicize information discrediting the 1984 Nicaraguan elections. Later, IBC's role was expanded to include organizing speaking tours and press conferences for contra leaders, conducting media-related services for the Office of Public Diplomacy (including "white propaganda," i.e., favorable publicity), and building a comprehensive computerized mailing list of some 3,300 names of groups, organizations, and individuals in a position to influence the debate over U.S. policy in Central America.

During this same period IBC received hundreds of thousands of dollars worth of contracts from the National Endowment for the Preservation of Liberty (NEPL). Some of these funds were spent on its public relations tasks, but others were transferred to the infamous Lake Resources from which Oliver North, Richard Secord, and Albert Hakim drew funds for support of the contras at a time when Congressional funds had been cut off. Richard Miller of IBC was indicted along with Carl R. "Spitz" Channel, conservative head of NEPL, for defrauding the U.S. government.

Democracy and Foreign Policy

Albert O. Hirschman, an economist known for his insightful views on Latin America, once articulated some fundamental truths about the nature of a democratic society. Political debate in democracies is always difficult, he argued, but becomes impossible when citizens lose two kinds of what Hirschman called "uncertainties." One necessary uncertainty in a democracy is about the course of policy-making. Activist members of the society must believe at some level that present policy is not the policy for all time and be willing to exercise patience until the next institutional opportunity is provided for altering the direction of policy. "One senses," Hirschman wrote, "that a society whose activist members are so sure of where they stand, and so immune to outside argument, may find it difficult to abide by the democratic process."[6]

A second kind of uncertainty concerns citizen attitudes at the mass level. Hirschman believes that "a genuine democratic political process implies that many of the people participating in it have only an approximate and somewhat uncertain initial opinion on various issues of public policy."[7] This uncertainty combines a lack of commitment to an inflexible, *a priori* position with a willingness to deliberate about the proper course to pursue. Taken together, these two "uncertainty" principles of democracy imply that democratic policy-making requires a tentativeness about whether the correct solutions to all current problems can be ascertained in advance of democratic debate of them, and patience on the part of activists to wait for their preferred policies to prevail.

Judged by Hirschman's standard, this review of the state of the debate on Central America in the 1980s gives some cause for alarm. The relative confusion and ignorance about basic issues on the part of the mass public, while regrettable on one level, also meant that they remained open to the empathetic deliberation prescribed by Hirschman. Members of the attentive public and opinion makers could have accepted the challenge of educating their fellow citizens to the importance of the debate over Central America in ways that would have equipped them to reach their own conclusions based on an understanding of opposing points of view.

Unfortunately, the 1980s will be recorded as a decade marked by the stridency of the foreign policy debate and partisan recrimination on Central America among elites. Although espousing nonpartisanship at times, some elements of the left/liberal lobby on Central America appeared to believe that their best tactic for mobilizing opposition to an administration policy they found dangerous and immoral was to attempt to polarize the public. By presenting the issues of Central America in stark terms of human rights versus support for the restoration of dictatorship and continued repression, some groups opposed to administration policy hoped to galvanize a "mass movement that tears so deeply into domestic social stability that Reagan cries 'uncle'. . . ."8 Frustrated that this did not happen, some debated whether the "low-intensity conflict" doctrine of U.S. counterinsurgency requires a new "low-intensity" political strategy for mobilizing and maintaining opposition to U.S. government foreign policy.9

Conservative lobbies on Central America adopted their own polarizing tactics in the battle for public opinion on Central America: to make the "Red Scare" concrete in the form of millions of refugees streaming across U.S. borders unless Communism is stopped in Central America by adherence to the Monroe Doctrine, renunciation of the Kennedy-Khrushchev accords barring an invasion of Cuba, and massive aid to the contras and El Salvador. Retired U.S. Army Brigadier General Albion W. Knight, Jr., in a fundraising appeal for the United States Defense Committee, put the argument directly:

> . . . if we allow the Communists to succeed, almost *two and a half million refugees* would stream out of Central America alone.
>
> *With an average cost to the American taxpayer of some $4,500 per refugee the yearly bill to the American taxpayer would be $10 billion.*
>
> That's just the tax bill.
>
> Think of the cost in human suffering to these poor people, the overwhelming number of whom speak no English, who are being forced to leave their homes and the land they love.
>
> Think of the uprooted families, the social problems they will face trying to become Americanized and the difficulties the United States will have trying to create new jobs.

Some people would say America should just keep the refugees out.

How could that be done?

A Communist country would set up machine guns and land mines and use poison gas to kill anyone who tried to come across the border.

But in America, based upon present State Department policies, we would just capture them and send them back to Mexico.

The next day they would try to sneak across the border again.

And again! And again! And again!

Until finally they would slip past our Border Patrol. The simple fact is that the right and moral solution is to provide now the needed military supplies and training to pro-American forces in Central America so that they can stop the Communist cancer from spreading so there will not be any refugees.

. . . it's also the least expensive thing to do.[10]

Appeals such as these were often echoed by administration spokespersons themselves.

Why was Central America so polarized and polarizing? Curiously, it may be because both right and left used Central America to play out ideological convictions that they could not express in the United States proper. Some argued that the right was "given" Central America at the beginning of the Reagan administration as an area where it could exercise its ideology without fear of drastic consequences. Even the greatest hawks in the Pentagon have concluded that the Soviet Union implicitly recognizes Central America as being in the U.S. sphere of influence and that the Soviets will refrain from frontal challenges to the United States in the region. This means, paradoxically, that no restraint on rhetoric or action by conservatives need apply because an ultimate confrontation with the Soviets is improbable. Policy motivated by ideology that might bring quick response from the Soviets or Soviet allies in the Middle East or Asia can be applied to Central America without apparent cost.

Part of the opposition to Reagan's policies saw Central America as another chance to "defeat U.S. imperialism" in a more profound and lasting way than it was "defeated" in Vietnam. It viewed the struggle for an agenda of radical reform at home as one with the conflict in Central America: "Though we are organizing at a *different* point in the global system than the people of Central America, our society is nevertheless torn by the same crisis."[11] Frustrated by its own inability to restructure U.S. society and politics along lines it finds desirable, the left looks to events in the Third World to mobilize forces for change in the United States.

A view of Central American policy inspired by Albert Hirschman's "uncertainties" would argue that no policy toward Central America will be successful or of great benefit to Central Americans if it is not sustainable over a long period. In a democracy this means that many people, from very different regions, walks of life, and political persuasions must come together in rough agreement. Two sets of "ideo-lobbies" shouting alternate white and black versions of the same reality to a largely uninformed public does not encourage that slight hesitancy that needs to exist in a democratic society about whether there is a single best answer to the Central American conundrum. Yet neither the Reagan administration and its supporters nor many of its critics acted as if they believed in this fundamental tenet of democracy.

The consensus on foreign policy currently lacking in the United States is unlikely to be restored soon. Meanwhile, foreign policy will be subjected to the same pulling and tugging by interested parties that characterizes domestic policy. The United States has so far survived the costs of democratic debate of domestic policy by acknowledging the need for compromise. A similar application of democratic politics to foreign policy may be the best substitute the nation is likely to encounter to replace the post–World War II consensus that prevailed in a simpler time.

Notes

1. Focus groups are structured conversations by a trained facilitator with ten to twelve individuals chosen to fit a demographic profile of age, sex, education, race, political affiliation, etc. They are not scientific in the way polls are, but often give a more nuanced view of why individuals hold the opinions they do. They also offer members of the group the opportunity to listen to the views of their fellow citizens and respond to them.
2. Mark Rovner, "Trouble at Our Doorstep: Public Attitudes and Public Policy on Central America (Washington, D.C.: Roosevelt Center for American Policy Studies, 1987).
3. Marc Cooper, "Whitewashing Duarte, U.S. Reporting on El Salvador," NACLA *Report on the Americas* (January/March 1986): 7–10.

4. Daniel James, *El Salvador: A Case History of U.S. Media Influence upon Public Attitudes toward Central America* (Washington, D.C.: Washington Institute for Values in Public Policy, 1985). Daniel James is a journalist who has been covering Central America since 1954 when he wrote a book heralding the CIA-engineered coup in Guatemala called *Red Design for the Americas: Guatemalan Prelude.* The Washington Institute for Values in Public Policy is funded by the Rev. Sun Yung Moon's organization. James's conclusions are based on pieces in the *New York Times, Washington Post, Newsweek,* ABC, and NBC, published or aired between October 16, 1979 and October 15, 1982.

5. Mark Falcoff, "The Apple of Discord, Central America in U.S. Domestic Politics," in *Rift and Revolution, The Central American Imbroglio,* Howard J. Wiarda, ed. (Washington, D.C.: American Enterprise Institute, 1984), pp. 360–81.

6. Albert O. Hirschman, "On Democracy in Latin America," *New York Review of Books* (April 10, 1986), p. 41.

7. Ibid., p. 42.

8. Paul Martin, "No More Vietnams, Old Slogan, New Vision," NACLA *Report on the Americas* 20, no. 4 (July/August 1986): 10.

9. In addition to Martin's article, see also Sara Miles, "The Real War: Low-Intensity Conflict in Central America," ibid. 20, no. 2 (April/May 1986): 17–48.

10. Letter, United States Defense Committee, (no date, 1986), p. 2. Emphasis in the original.

11. Martin, "No More Vietnams," p. 10.

Index

Abrams, Elliott, 57
Agriculture, 5
Alliance for Progress, 33–34
Alvarez Martínez, Gustavo
    (Honduran general), 71, 123–24
Americas Watch Committee, 84
Amnesty International, 84
Anaya, Herbert, 68
Aníbal Guevara, Angel (Guatemalan
    general), 86
Arbenz, Jacobo, 31, 84
Arce, Bayardo, 105
Arevalo, Juan José, 30
Argentina, 13–14
Arias, Oscar (Costa Rican president),
    59, 79, 81, 108, 129, 141
Arms-for-hostages deal. *See* Iran-
    contra affair
Assassinations, 63, 84, 86, 87, 150
Azcona Hoyo, José, 70

Baker, Lorenzo Dow, 16
Banana republic, 18
Banana trade, 16–18
Banking system, 130–31
Barnes, Michael, 149
"Beans and bullets" program, 132
Bertke, Marlene (Benedictine nun),
    142
Bitter Fruit, 16–18
"Black Legend," 1

Boland Amendment, 54–55, 56–57
Bolívar, Simón, 9–10, 19
Bonilla, Manuel, 17
Bonior, David, 155
Bonner, Raymond, 145
Boston Fruit Company, 16
Bradley, Bill, 152
Buckley, William F., Jr., 21
Buendía, Aureliano, 9
Buhl, Cindy, 141
Bunau-Varilla, Phillipe, 20

Cabot, John Moors, 31
Cabot, Thomas, 31
Callejas, Rafael Leonardo, 70
Campesinos, 62
Cárdenas Vargas, René, 68
Carías Andino, Tiburcio, 27
Caribbean Basin, 100
Carolinas Interfaith Task Force on
    Central America, 142
Carpio Nicolle, Jorge, 87–88
Carter administration, 86, 113, 132,
    142; Nicaraguan policy, 51
Casey, William (CIA director), 56,
    57, 58
Castro, Fidel (Cuban leader), 103;
    armed struggle strategy, 38
Catholic church, 1, 3, 10;
    progressivism, 35–36. *See also*
    Churches and church groups

Catholic Relief Services, 142
Caudillo, 10
CCC. *See* Committee of Campesino Unity
Center for National Policy, 142
Central America: churches and, 140–43; conservatives versus liberals, 8–11; contemporary (1960s and 1970s), 33–38; depression, 27; founding of, 3–6; history, lessons of, 41–44; land tenure pattern, 4–5; liberals, 24–25; media coverage, 145–48; social groups, 4–5; wartime partnership with U.S., 29–30. *See also* specific countries
Central American Common Market, 39–40
Central American Peace Plan of August 7, 1987, 68, 79
Central Intelligence Agency (CIA), 156
Cerezo, Vinicio (Guatemalan president), 84, 87–88, 133
Chamorro Cardenal, Pedro Joaquín, 49
Channel, Carl R. ("Spitz"), 157
Chapman, Mike, 141
Chauncey, George, 143
Christiani, Alfredo, 68
Churches and church groups, 140–43, 153–54; Impact '88, 140. *See also* Catholic church
Church World Service, 142–43
CISPES. *See* Committee in Solidarity with the People of El Salvador
Civil war following independence, 9–11
Coelho, Tony, 155
Coffee growers, xviii–xx, 15
Cold War, 30

Colombia, 14; Panama Canal in, 19–20
Colonial heritage, 5–6
Committee in Solidarity with the People of El Salvador (CISPES), 153, 155
Committee of Campesino Unity (CCC), 88
Communism, 110–11, 153, 158. *See also* Marxism-Leninism
CONSUFA. *See* Supreme Council of the Armed Forces (Honduras)
Contadora peace proposals, 80–83
Contras, 51–53, 59, 128, 137, 141; human rights violations, 151; U.S. aid, 108, 139, 151–52, 154. *See also* Iran-contra affair
Cooper, Marc, 145–56
Costa Rica, 7, 75–79, 83; banking system, 130–31; development, 25–27; economy, 78, 130; elections, 75, 79; highways, 75; key facts, 83–84; neutrality, 129; Nicaragua and, 78–79, 129; population, 26; revolution of 1948, 77–78; Sandinistas and, 78; social policies, 77; U.S. and, 79, 128–31
Countdown 1987, 154
Criollos, 6
Cruz, Arturo, 50, 52
Cuba, 19, 38, 95, 99, 111; Platt Amendment, 19

Darwin's theory of evolution, 15
D'Aubuisson, Roberto, 66–67
Davila, Miguel (Honduran president), 17
Death squads, 37, 65, 147–48
De Lauro, Rosa, 154
de Lesseps, Ferdinand, 19

Democracy and foreign policy, 157–60

Democratic Revolutionary Front (FDR), 64

Depression, 27

DeYoung, Karen, 145

Díaz, Adolfo, 23

Directory of Central American Organizations, 153

Dodd, Christopher, 149, 154, 155

Dominican Republic, 34

Domino theory, 101, 103

Duarte, José Napoléon, 64, 66, 67, 82, 116, 119, 120, 121, 145

Dulles, Allen (head of CIA), 31

Dulles, John Foster (U.S. secretary of state), 31

Earthquakes, 67, 88

Economy, 42, 60, 78, 89

Education, 25, 63

Eisenhower administration, 103

El Dorado, 3

Elections, 75, 79, 87, 104

El Salvador, 7, 36, 43, 61–69, 126, 149–50, 153, 155; airport, 61; ARENA party, 66, 67, 68; assassinations, 150; Central American Peace Plan of August 7, 1987, effect of, 68; civil war, 64–65; Coprefa, 147; death squads, 65, 83, 147–48, 151; earthquake, 67; education, 63; election of 1972, 64; guerrilla movement, 38; health care, 63; human rights violations, 151; key facts, 69; land reform program, 62; media coverage, 145–48; peasant uprising, 27; population, 61; reformist junta, 65; San Martin del Campo, xvii–xviii; Soccer War, 39, 72, 115; U.S. aid, 65–66, 67, 126; U.S. policy debate, 108–13, 113–21; Vietnam, similarities to, 117–18

Esquipulas II peace agreement, 81, 107–8, 151

Falkland/Malvinas Islands, 13, 95

Farabundo Martí, Augusto, 27, 64

Farabundo Martí Liberation Front (FMLN), 27, 64, 155

FDR. See Democratic Revolutionary Front

Federal Bureau of Investigation (FBI), 155

Ferdinand VII (king of Spain), 6

Figueres Ferrer, José ("Pepe"), 77

FMLN. See Farabundo Martí Liberation Front

Foley, Thomas S., 141

Forces of National Liberation, 77

Foreign Affairs, 28

France, 13

FSLN. See Sandinista National Liberation Front

Fueros, 10

García Márquez, Gabriel, 8–9, 11–12

Gomez, Frank, 156

Good Neighbor Policy, 28–29

Gramajo, Hector (Guatemalan defense minister), 134

Great Britain, 1–3, 13, 95

Gringos, 12, 44n

Guatemala, 7, 30–33, 36, 84–90; accords (see Esquipulas II peace agreement); agrarian reform law, 31; assassinations, 84, 86, 87; "Beans and Rifles" strategy, 86; CIA in, 32; communism, 30–31;

earthquake, 88; economic aid, 134; economy, 89; elections, 31, 87; guerrilla movements, 37–38; key facts, 89–90; military activity, 88–89; reformism, 30; U.S. policy debate, 132–35

Guatemala: A Government Program of Political Murder, 84

Guatemala News in Brief, 84

Guerrilla warfare, 23, 37, 63–64, 67–68, 86, 119, 132–33, 146–47; training base, 38; U.S. policy debate, 114–16

Haciendas, 44n

Haig, Alexander (U.S. secretary of state), 149, 152

Hakim, Albert, 56, 58, 157

Hall, Fawn, 55, 58

Harkin, Tom, 149, 155

Health care, 63

Hernández Martínez, Maximiliano (Salvadoran general), 27

Hidalgo (Father), 6

Highways, 75

Hirschman, Albert O., 157

Holmes, Mary Hayes, 142

Honduras, 7, 69–75, 115; elections, 70; key facts, 74–75; Soccer War, 39, 72, 115; U.S. and, 72–74, 122–28; U.S. Regional Military Training Center, 72, 73

HRAs. *See* Human rights activists

Human rights activists (HRAs), 102–4, 110–13, 114–21, 118, 120, 121, 123, 124–25, 126–28, 129, 131, 134; stereotypical description of, 97

Human rights violations, 151

Hyde, Henry J., 141

Iklé, Fred C., 122

Impact '88, 140

Independence, 6–8

Indians, 3–4, 6, 11, 30, 37, 85, 86, 132

Inouye, Daniel (U.S. senator), 57–58

Intermarriage, 4

International Business Communications (IBC), 156

Iran-contra affair, 54–59; hearings, 156; Select Committee to Investigate Covert Arms Transactions with Iran, 55; Select Committee on Secret Military Assistance to Iran and the Nicaraguan Opposition, 55; Tower Commission report, 55–56

Iturbide (Mexican general), 7

James, Daniel, 146, 161 n4

John Paul II (pope), 36

Johnson, Lyndon Baines (U.S. president), 34

Keith, Minor, 16

Kennedy, John F. (U.S. president), 33, 91

Kennedy, Ted, 155

Kennedy administration, 99

Khrushchev, Nikita (Soviet leader), 99

Kissinger, Henry (U.S. secretary of state), 148–49, 152

Knight, Albion W., Jr. (U.S. brigadier general), 158–59

Kundanis, George, 141

Ladinos, 6

Land reform, 62

Latifundio, 44n

LeoGrande, William M., 140, 141

Liberals, 24–25

Lincoln, Abraham, 14

Linder, Benjamin, 153

"Living museum" concept, 11
Lodge, Henry Cabot (U.N.
  ambassador), 31
López Reyes, Walter (Honduran
  general), 71, 72, 124
Lucas García, Romeo, 86

Manifest Destiny, 14, 45n
Mao Zedong, 132
Marxism-Leninism, 101, 103–4,
  105, 110, 129; See also
  Communism
Maryknoll Sisters, FBI surveillance
  of, 155
Matta Ballesteros, Juan Ramón, 74
McBrayer, Jerry, 140, 143
McCurdy, Dave, 141
McFarlane, Robert, 56, 57
Media coverage, influence of, 145–
  48
Meese, Edwin (U.S. attorney
  general), 54, 55
Mejía Víctores, Oscar (Guatemalan
  brigadier general), 87, 133
Mestizo, 4
Mexico, 14, 103; Chiapas, 7;
  independence, movement for, 7;
  Texas annexed from, 14
Michel, Robert H. 137
Middle class, 5
MIG aircraft, 99
Military: aid, 110; changes during
  the twentieth century, 34–35;
  training, 72, 73
Miller, Richard, 156, 157
Minifundio, 44n
Mining, 5
Monge, Luis Alberto (Costa Rican
  president), 78, 79, 128–29
Monroe, James (U.S. president), 13
Monroe Doctrine, 13; Roosevelt
  Corollary, 18

Moon, Sun Yung, 161n
Motley, 106–7, 117–18
Moyers, Bill, 137
Murders. *See* Assassinations

National Endowment for the
  Preservation of Liberty (NEPL),
  156
National Liberation Party (PLN), 77
National security analysts (NSAs),
  105–8, 110–13, 114–21, 117, 118,
  119, 120, 122–23, 124, 126, 127,
  128, 130, 131, 134; stereotypical
  description, 93–94, 96–97
National Security Council:
  "Summary Paper" on Central
  America (1982), 144
NEPL. *See* National Endowment for
  the Preservation of Liberty
Network in Solidarity with the
  People of Guatemala (NISGUA),
  153
New York Times, 145
Nicaragua, 7, 13–14, 22–23, 27–28,
  43, 47–53, 59–61, 98–104, 149,
  150–51, 152; Carter
  administration's policy, 51;
  Catholic Church, 36; contras (*see*
  Contras); Costa Rica and, 78–79,
  129; economy, 60; elections, 104;
  Esquipulas II peace agreement,
  108; Iran-contra affair, 54; key
  facts, 60–61; Matagalpa, xviii–xx;
  National Guard, 50; Panama Canal
  and, 19–20; press coverage, 148;
  private sector, xviii–xx; Reagan
  administration's policy, 51;
  Sandinista movement (*see*
  Sandinista movement); U.S.
  involvement in, 22, 52–53;
  Witness for Peace volunteers sent
  to, 142

Nicaragua Network, 153
NISGUA. *See* Network in Solidarity
  with the People of Guatemala
Nobel Peace Prize, 79
North America, founding of, 3–5
North American Congress on Latin
  America (NACLA), 145
North, Oliver (U.S. lieutenant
  colonel), 53, 55, 57, 58, 156
NSAs. *See* National security analysts
  (NSAs)
Nuclear weapons, 99, 102

OAS. *See* Organization of American
  States
Obando y Bravo, Miguel (Cardinal),
  108
Obey, David R., 141
O'Donnell, Kirk, 142
Oil shortages (1970s), 39, 40
One Hundred Years of Solitude, 8–9,
  11–12
Organization of American States
  (OAS), 50–51
Ortega, Daniel (Nicaraguan
  president), 52, 59, 82

Panama, 13–14
Panama Canal, 19–22; treaty, 20–21
Paraguay, 14
Pax Americana, 141
Peace proposals, 68, 79, 80–83
Penados del Barrio, Próspero
  (Guatemalan archbishop), 88
Peninsulars, 6–7
Peru, 13
Pezzullo, Lawrence (U.S.
  ambassador), 113
Plantations, 5, 7
Platt Amendment, 19
Playboy, 145
PLN. *See* National Liberation Party

Pocahontas, 4
Poindexter, John (U.S. rear admiral),
  55, 56, 57, 58
Policy-making, 157
Political instability, 41–42
Positivism, 14–15
Prensa, La, 49, 53, 106
Pureza de sangre, 4

Reagan, Ronald (U.S. president), 21,
  105, 109–10, 117, 149; Iran-
  contra affair, 56; speeches, 155–
  56
Reagan administration, 53, 66, 81,
  108, 113, 114, 137, 144, 145, 152;
  "coercive diplomacy", 107; critics,
  140; Iran-contra affair. (*see* Iran-
  contra affair); Nicaraguan policy,
  51; opposition to, 149, 153
Reagan Doctrine, 149
*Red Design for the Americas:
  Guatemalan Prelude*, 161n
"Red Scare," 158
Regalado (Honduran general), 124
Revell, Oliver B., 155
Ríos Montt, Efraín (Guatemalan
  president), 86–87, 132–33
Romero, Carlos Humberto, 64
Romero, Oscar (archbishop), 36, 66,
  142
Roosevelt, Franklin Delano (U.S.
  President), 28–29, 103
Roosevelt, Theodore (U.S.
  president), 18–22
Roosevelt Center "focus groups,"
  139, 143–44, 160n
Roosevelt Corollary to the Monroe
  Doctrine, 18
Rough Riders, 18

"Salvospeak," 117
Sanctuary movement, 154
Sandinista movement, xviii, 49–53,

80–81, 82, 113, 122, 128, 129; "free fire zones," 53; press coverage, 148; relationship with Costa Rica, 78; U.S., relations with, 50–53; U.S. policy debate, 105–8
Sandinista National Liberation Front (FSLN), 23, 49, 105
Sandino, Augusto Cesar, 22, 23
"Scorched-earth policy", 86
Secord, Richard, 56, 58
Shiraa, Al, 54
Shultz, George (U.S. secretary of state), 58–59, 124
Soccer War, 39, 72, 115
Social reforms, 29
Soldier of Fortune, 117
Somoza, Anastasio, 23, 27–28, 29, 50; opposition to, 47–50
Somoza, "Tachito," 38
Soviet-Cuban Connection in Central America and the Caribbean, The, 100
Soviet Union, 38, 99, 100, 102, 109–12, 115–16, 159
Spain: history of involvement in Central America, 1–3; limited monarchy, 6
Stepp, Laura Sessions, 143
Studds, Gerry, 149
Suázo Córdoba, Roberto (Honduran president), 70, 71, 125
Supreme Council of the Armed Forces (Honduras) (CONSUFA), 71

Tanenhaus, Marta Iris, 59
TECNICA, 153
Time, 88
Tower, John, 55

Ubico, Jorge (Guatemalan general), 27, 30

Ungo, Guillermo, 64, 65, 68
Union of American Hebrew Congregations, 142
United Auto Workers, FBI surveillance of, 155
United Fruit Company (UFCO), 16–18, 31–32
United Provinces of Central America, 7
United States: aid, 41, 65–66, 67, 73, 108, 139, 151–52, 154; Alliance for Progress, 33–34; annexation of Texas from Mexico, 14; congressional policy debate, 148–52; contras, aid to, 108, 139, 151–52, 154; Costa Rica, relations with, 79; Defense Guidance, 95–96; East-West problems, 108–9; El Salvador, aid to, 65–66, 67, 126; Executive Order 12333, 156; FBI surveillance, 155; foreign policy and democracy, 157–60; foreign policy initiatives, 13; Honduran relations, 72–74; hostility towards, 127; Iran-contra affair (*see* Iran-contra affair); Latin America's perception of, 11–12; "low-intensity conflict (LIC)," 40–41; national interests defined, 95–96; National Security Council (*see* National Security Council); Nicaraguan relations, 52–53; North-South issues, 109; "Potomac fever," 91, 93; public opinion, 138–39; role in Central America, 42–44; Sandinstas and, 50–53, 98–104; vital interests of, 95–96, 99; volunteer brigades, 153; War Powers Act, 148; wartime partnership with Latin America, 29–30; Washington, D.C. described, 91, 93. *See also*

names of specific administrations
Uruguay, 13–14, 131
U.S. Catholic Conference, 141

Vendepatrias, 127
Vides Casanova (Salvadoran
    general), 120
Vietnam: effect on U.S. policy in
    Central America, 96, 148;
    similarities to, 101, 117–18
Vital interests of U.S., 95–96, 99
Volunteer brigades, 153

Walker, William, 14
Walsh, Lawrence (special
    prosecutor), 55, 58

War Powers Act, 148
Washington Office on Latin
    America, 154
Washington Post, 145
White House Outreach Group on
    Central America, 144
"Whitewashing Duarte," 145
Wilson, Woodrow (U.S. president),
    28
Witness for Peace, 142, 154
Wright, Jim, 57, 59

Zamora, Mario, 65
Zamora, Rubén, 65, 68
Zelaya, President, 22
Zemurray, Samuel, 16